My Read at Home Book

3

Jim Halligan   John Newman

Published by

CJ Fallon
Ground Floor – Block B
Liffey Valley Office Campus
Dublin 22

ISBN 978-0-7144-1828-5

First Edition March 2012
This Reprint September 2015

© Jim Halligan and John Newman

Design © CJ Fallon

Acknowledgements

The publishers gratefully acknowledge the following for permission to reproduce copyright material.

Mice, by Rose Fyleman. Reprinted by permission of the The Society of Authors as the Literary Representative of the Estate of Rose Fyleman. *Schoolitis*, by Brian Patten © Brian Patten. Reproduced by permission of the author c/o Rogers, Coleridge & White Ltd., 20 Powis Mews, London W11 1JN.

Every effort has been made to secure permission to reproduce copyright material in this book. If the publishers have inadvertently overlooked any copyright holders, however, they will be pleased to come to a suitable arrangement with them at the earliest opportunity.

All rights reserved.
No part of this publication may be reproduced or transmitted, in any form or by any means, electronic, mechanical, photocopying or otherwise, without the prior written permission of the publisher.

Printed in Ireland by
Turner Print Group
Street
ford

Introduction

The aim of *My Read at Home Book 3* is to develop reading fluency and comprehension skills by encouraging daily independent reading *at home*. The book consists of 120 single page units, arranged into 30 sections (one per week of the school year). Each page (or 'day') is a stand-alone piece, with a variety of styles and themes to appeal to all tastes and interests. Genres such as fact, fiction, letter writing, poetry, humour, history, geography, nature and legend are all included. A key element of promoting literacy (i.e. daily practice) is achieved effectively.

How To Use *My Read at Home Book 3*

- Children are assigned one page of reading for homework each day of the week except Friday.

- The children read the assigned page at home. Confident readers will manage this without help. However, parents/guardians should be encouraged to help less fluent readers by reading *with them* (paired reading).

- Children should be encouraged to pre-read the **Check-up** questions on each page, to help their recall.

- The teacher will then **check** the reading the following day by **orally** asking the **Check-up** questions.

- Optional: Most passages in *My Read at Home Book 3* lead easily into class discussion. This is to be encouraged to help develop the **oral language skills** of the children.

Contents

Week	Day		Genre	Page
1	1	Daydreamer	Fiction	1
	2	Chickens	Fact	2
	3	Pancake Batter	Recipe	3
	4	Henry Ford	History	4
2	1	Fallen Hero	Fiction	5
	2	Sand	Fact	6
	3	Special Days	Fact	7
	4	Grace O'Malley	History	8
3	1	Pet Day	Fiction	9
	2	Postcards From Where?	Geography	10
	3	Summer Camp	Advertisement	11
	4	Henry VIII	History	12
4	1	The New Girl	Fiction	13
	2	Shark!	Nature	14
	3	A Recycling Song For Your School	Song	15
	4	Marco Polo	History	16
5	1	Love and Hate	Fiction	17
	2	Cats	Fact	18
	3	Mice	Poetry	19
	4	George Stephenson	History	20
6	1	The Sea Cave	Fiction	21
	2	Blue Planet	Fact	22
	3	Lost!	Fiction	23
	4	The Spirit of Saint Louis	History	24

Week	Day		Genre	Page
7	1	999	Fiction	25
	2	Cars	Fact	26
	3	Buns	Recipe	27
	4	John Logie Baird	History	28
8	1	In the Woods	Fiction	29
	2	Nuts and Seeds	Nature	30
	3	Hallowe'en Shopping List	Fiction	31
	4	Alice the Witch of Kilkenny	History	32
9	1	The Guitar Man	Fiction	33
	2	Under Your Feet!	Nature	34
	3	Polar Bears	Fact	35
	4	Louis Braille	History	36
10	1	A Letter to Say Sorry	Letter	37
	2	Squirrels	Nature	38
	3	Look at the Picture	Observation	39
	4	Cliffs of Moher	Geography	40
11	1	Pocket Genie	Fiction	41
	2	Sherpas	Fact	42
	3	A Sense of Smell	Science	43
	4	Hans Christian Andersen	Fact	44
12	1	A Boat Trip	Fiction	45
	2	Ring Ring	Fiction	46
	3	For Sale	Advertisement	47
	4	At the Gates	History	48
13	1	Wrong Number!	Fiction	49
	2	Daisies	Science	50
	3	Questions	Poetry	51
	4	Gone in Eight Minutes	Fact	52
14	1	Grow Your Own Monster	Fiction	53
	2	Chinese Dragons	History	54
	3	The Chuck Wagon Restaurant	Menu	55
	4	Monsters	Fact	56

CONTENTS

Week	Day		Genre	Page
15	1	The Little Thief	Fiction	57
	2	Down By The Sea	Science	58
	3	How to Make a Paper Aeroplane	Visual arts	59
	4	September 1847	History	60
16	1	The Snake	Fiction	61
	2	Blackbeard	History	62
	3	School Timetable	Poetry	63
	4	Setanta	Legend	64
17	1	Green Fingers	Fiction	65
	2	Frogs	Nature	66
	3	Oops!	Observation	67
	4	Aesop	Myth	68
18	1	Survivor	Fiction	69
	2	A Plant That Can Count?	Nature	70
	3	Dog	Poetry	71
	4	The Lost City of Atlantis	Legend	72
19	1	The Puppy Campaign	Fiction	73
	2	Ants	Nature	74
	3	Chocolate Rice Krispies Cakes	Recipe	75
	4	Bones	Nature	76
20	1	Cat Trouble	Fiction	77
	2	Cat and Mouse	Legend	78
	3	World Top Tens	Fact	79
	4	Carrauntoohill	Geography	80
21	1	Snow	Fiction	81
	2	Snakes	Nature	82
	3	Banana Bread	Recipe	83
	4	Christopher Columbus	History	84
22	1	Fireworks	Fiction	85
	2	Vikings	History	86
	3	The Best Garlic Bread Ever	Recipe	87
	4	Brian Boru	History	88

Week	Day		Genre	Page
23	1	Spoilt Girl	Fiction	89
	2	Footwear	Fact	90
	3	When Night Falls	Nature	91
	4	Rosa Parks	History	92
24	1	Lamb	Fiction	93
	2	Planets	Geography	94
	3	Postman on Sick Leave	Poetry	95
	4	Yuri Gagarin	History	96
25	1	Rules!	Rules	97
	2	Water, Water, Everywhere	Nature	98
	3	Schoolitis	Poetry	99
	4	William Tell	Legend	100
26	1	Greenland	Geography	101
	2	Travelling	Fact	102
	3	Tyrannosaurus Rex	Poetry	103
	4	Taj Mahal	History	104
27	1	Supergirl	Fiction	105
	2	Spiders	Nature	106
	3	Odd Jobs	Fact	107
	4	The Little Dutch Boy	Legend	108
28	1	Climbing the Wall	Fiction	109
	2	The Eiffel Tower	Fact	110
	3	Superman's Diary	Diary	111
	4	The World's Biggest Omelette	Fact	112
29	1	Dream Catcher	Fiction	113
	2	Lulu	Fiction	114
	3	The Sun	Geography	115
	4	The Lady of the Lamp	History	116
30	1	Up in a Cloud	Fiction	117
	2	Mines	Fact	118
	3	Animal World Records	Nature	119
	4	Dublin Zoo	Fact	120

CONTENTS

DAYDREAMER

Jim is not very good at listening to his teacher. However, he is a world champion at daydreaming. In class, Jim always looks wide awake. He seems to be listening to every word his teacher says. But if you look closely, you can see that his eyes are glazed over. If you could go inside his head, you would enter a very strange world indeed.

Inside his head, Jim is exploring strange, far away planets. He is fighting Jedi knights. In his daydreams, he is a superhero saving the world. In his imagination, he can talk to animals. He can fly high in the sky like a bird. His body might be sitting in the classroom, but his mind is far, far away. It is in a land of elephants with painted toenails swinging through the trees by their tails!

Most days, Jim cannot do his maths or understand his Irish homework because he has not been listening to his teacher. Is it any wonder that his teacher thinks to herself, 'He is a nice boy, but there is not much going on in that head of his!'

CHECK-UP

1. What is the name of the story?
2. What is Jim a world champion at?
3. What are his eyes like?
4. What is Jim in his daydreams?
5. Why does he not understand his Irish homework?

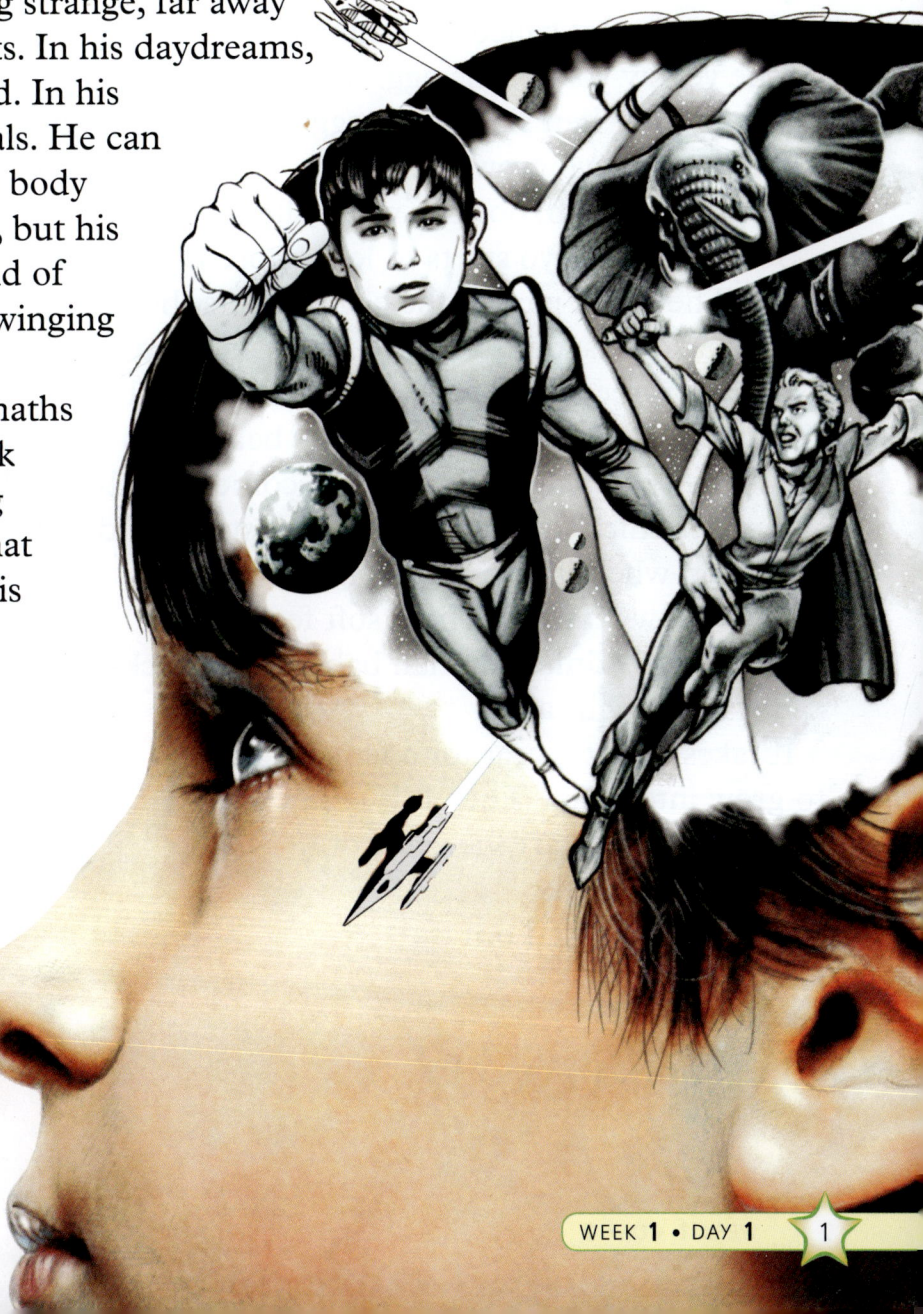

WEEK 1 • DAY 1

Chickens

A famous riddle asks the question: 'Which came first? The chicken or the egg?'

The problem is that chickens come out of eggs, and eggs come out of chickens!

A male chicken that is over one year old is called a **cock**. A female chicken that is over one year old is called a **hen**. Hens like to lay their eggs in a nest of straw, but anywhere warm will do. Inside the egg, the baby chicken is only a tiny dot called an **embryo**. The embryo feeds on the yellow yolk of the egg.

The mother hen sits on her eggs to keep them warm while the embryo grows inside the shell. The mother hen is said to be **brooding** when she does this.

Soon, the embryo starts to look more like a baby chick. The white part of the egg protects the growing baby chick. It is a bit like jelly and is called **albumen**.

It takes three weeks for the egg to hatch. The tiny chick has a special egg tooth on its beak. This helps it break the shell when it is ready to come into the world. When the chick first hatches, it is all sticky and wet. However, when it dries out, it has lovely, soft, fluffy, yellow feathers. These soft feathers are called **down**. Unlike human babies, the chicks can walk straight away.

It takes about a year for a female chick to grow into a hen. Then it is ready to lay eggs and start the cycle of life all over again!

Have you worked out the riddle yet?

CHECK-UP

1. What is a female chicken that is over one year old called?
2. What is the baby chick called when it is still only a tiny dot in the egg?
3. What is albumen?
4. How does the chick crack open the shell?
5. What are soft little feathers called?

Recipe
Pancake Batter

This is a recipe for delicious pancakes that you can make at home with your family.

Ingredients

For this recipe, you will need:
- 200g plain flour
- 4 eggs
- 30g sugar
- Pinch of salt
- ½ litre of milk

Preparation

1. Sieve the flour into a large bowl.
2. Beat the eggs into the flour (use an electric mixer or a wooden spoon).
3. Add the sugar and salt to the mixture.
4. Continue to beat it gently as you add the milk.
5. Cool the mixture (batter) in the fridge before using it.
6. Ask an adult to help you make your delicious pancakes.

CHECK-UP
1. What is the recipe for?
2. How much flour is needed in the recipe?
3. How many eggs are needed in the recipe?
4. What should you do with the batter before making the pancakes?
5. Why would you need an adult's help to cook the pancakes?

Henry Ford

Henry Ford was born in July 1863 in the USA. As a child, all he ever really wanted to do was invent things and do experiments. He used to take clockwork toys and clocks apart to see how they worked. When he was not working on the family farm, he would walk for half a day into the nearest town to look at the watchmaker at work.

When Henry was 17, he went to work in the city of Detroit. He got a job in a factory making railway wagons. However, his dream was to build a petrol car. He built his first car in his kitchen! He used to drive it around town and a big crowd would run after him in excitement. One day, a man ran out in front of him and was knocked down. The man was not badly hurt but it is thought to be the first car accident in America.

In 1903, Henry started a car-making company called the **Ford Motor Company**. The most popular car he designed was called the **Model T**. It was nicknamed the **Tin Lizzie**. The car was cheap and reliable. It was made on an **assembly line**. This meant that each worker became very skilled at a particular job. One would work on fitting doors, another on fitting seats, and so on. The Ford Motor Company made millions of Model T cars. Soon Henry was very rich and famous all over the world.

Henry Ford died in 1947 aged 83. Ford cars are still driven all over the world. Maybe your parents drive one?

> **CHECK-UP**
> 1 In what year and country was Henry Ford born?
> 2 As a child, what did Henry want to do?
> 3 What was his dream?
> 4 Where did he build his first car?
> 5 How old was Henry when he died?

Fallen Hero

Gary squeezed his eyes shut with the pain in his knee and his elbow. They hurt really badly and he had no one to blame but himself. It served him right, he supposed. No one had forced him to try to climb the big chestnut tree at the end of the school yard. It had been a stupid thing to do.

Oh, but what if he had managed it? He had been sure he could do it. He was the best climber in the school. If he had pulled it off, they would have been talking about it for years. Well, for days, anyway.

Okay, so the tree was out of bounds. It was as tall as the church down the road. No one had been able to even get up into its first branch before. But it was there! He had to try!

And he had tried. But now he was lying on the ground with the knee out of his trousers and blood pouring from a nasty cut on his elbow. It had not gone well. And now he could see Miss Kenny coming straight towards him across the yard. Oh goody!

CHECK-UP
1 What was the boy's name?
2 What kind of tree had he tried to climb?
3 Why had he tried to climb the tree?
4 What had he done to his trousers?
5 Who was coming to help him?

WEEK 2 • DAY 1

Sand

Sand on the beach is great fun to play with. In the summer time, people love to go to the beach and play on the sand. They dig holes, make sandcastles and lie on it to sunbathe. However, sand is also very useful to people.

Grains of sand were once rocks and stones. Over many millions of years, the sea has worn down these rocks into tiny grains of sand. Humans use sand in lots of ways.

Sandbags are canvas sacks filled with sand. In battles, soldiers hide behind sandbags to stop bullets hitting them. Sandbags are also very useful for holding back floods by acting as a barrier.

Sand is often used by builders. They mix it with cement and water to make concrete. Some crops, such as watermelons, peaches and peanuts, need to grow in sandy soil. Sand is even used on golf courses in bunkers.

Sand on the beach is great for playing with and sunbathing on. This is because sand gets hot very quickly in the sun. It can even burn your bare feet. However, sand loses heat very quickly too. That is why it gets so cold in deserts at night.

Perhaps the most amazing thing about sand is that it can be made into glass.

CHECK-UP

1. Why do soldiers use sandbags?
2. What crops need sandy soil?
3. What do builders use sand for?
4. What happens to sand in the sun?
5. What amazing thing is made out of sand?

Special Days

Month	Date	Name of Day
January	1st	New Year's Day
February	1st	St Brigid's Day
	14th	St Valentine's Day
March	17th	St Patrick's Day
March/April	4th Sunday in Lent	Mother's Day
April	1st	April Fool's Day
May	1st	May Day
June	20th or 21st	Midsummer Day
	3rd Sunday in June	Father's Day
July		Summer holidays – every day is special!
August		More summer holidays
September		Back to school
October	31st	Hallowe'en
November	1st	All Hallows' Day
December	25th	Christmas Day
	26th	St Stephen's Day
	31st	New Year's Eve

CHECK-UP

1. How many special days are in this list?
2. How many special days are there in December?
3. How many of the days are named after saints?
4. What special day is in October?
5. Which is your favourite month? Why?

WEEK 2 • DAY 3

Grace O'Malley

Grace O'Malley lived in Ireland about 500 years ago. Her father was a great chief who sailed the seas around Ireland. He would fill his ship with all sorts of things and trade them to make money. Sometimes he acted like a pirate and stole from other ships. He had castles in County Mayo and was very important. Grace wanted to be just like her father.

When she was young, Grace dreamed of being a sailor. However, when she asked her father if she could sail on his ship, he laughed at her. He said that a girl could never go to sea or be the captain of a ship. Well, Grace wanted to show him that she could! She cut off all her lovely long hair so that she looked like a boy. Then she sneaked onto her father's ship. When he found Grace later, he knew that she really wanted to be like him. He then started to teach her all that he knew about ships and the sea.

When she was older, Grace became the chief of her family (or clan). She was the best leader they ever had, even better than her father. She wasn't a bit of a pirate. She was a LOT of a pirate! Any ship she found at sea had to give her some of its goods, or else! Everybody was scared of her.

Grace and her ships are long gone now but you can still see her castle in Mayo. People there still talk about Grace, the Pirate Queen.

CHECK-UP
1. What was Grace O'Malley's father?
2. What did her father do when she said she wanted to be a sailor?
3. How did her father help her become a good sailor?
4. What happened when she was older?
5. What can you still see today that used to belong to Grace?

Pet Day

After the summer holidays, we got a new teacher called Mr Hoppy. There was also a new pupil in our class called Ravi.

Mr Hoppy was a big, loud man whom we all liked straight away. Ravi was from India. He was quiet and serious. However, he did smile when one day Mr Hoppy said,

'I want you to bring in your pets tomorrow and talk about them to the class.'

The next day was a bit crazy in class. I brought in my pet turtles, Orla brought in her pet snake and there were three pet dogs barking at four pet cats.

When Ravi arrived, Mr Hoppy called out, 'Have you no pet, lad?'

'Yes, I have,' said Ravi politely. 'He's outside.'

'Well bring him in!' laughed Mr Hoppy.

But Ravi told him that it was not a good idea.

'Is it a man-eating tiger?' asked Mr Hoppy.

'No,' said Ravi. 'He is very gentle.'

'Then bring him in!' insisted Mr Hoppy.

'Bring him in, Ravi,' we all shouted.

So, in the end, Ravi did bring his pet into the classroom.

'Come come Amar,' he called, and his pet elephant crashed through the classroom door, taking half of the wall with it.

CHECK-UP

1. What was the new teacher's name?
2. What type of pet did Orla bring in?
3. Why did Ravi not want to bring his pet into the classroom?
4. Did Ravi's pet fit through the door of the classroom? Explain your answer.
5. What do you think happened next?

Postcards From Where?

Can you work out the cities from where these postcards were sent?

Cork   London   Amsterdam
New York   Cairo   Paris

1 Having a wonderful time here. Saw the Eiffel Tower and the Arc de Triomphe. Hope to go and see the Mona Lisa tomorrow in the Louvre. Might even work up the courage to try to eat snails!
See you soon. Sam.

2 What a fantastic city! So many people. So many things to see. Was at the top of the Empire State Building yesterday. Took a boat trip to see Ellis Island and the Statue of Liberty today. Fed some pigeons in Central Park.
Love to all, Jenny.

3 What a friendly place. Lots of people riding around on bicycles. Visited the Anne Frank house. It was very sad. Took a boat trip along the canals. Saw a really old windmill. It was cool. Going to see some Van Gogh paintings tomorrow. Promise I will bring you home some cheese and some tulip bulbs.
Tom.

4 Wow! The pyramids really blew my mind! The Sphinx is amazing. It is really hot here. We are going to take a trip up the Nile tomorrow. Planning to go and see the Valley of the Kings also.
Love Derek and Kate.

5 Lots to see here. Went to the Tower to see the Crown jewels. Then we went to see Big Ben. Got to see the Rosetta Stone in the museum, along with the Roman emperor Tiberius's sword. Cool or what? Going to Madame Tussauds tomorrow.
Jack.

6 Having a ball here on the banks of the River Lee. Did lots of shopping in Patrick Street. Bought some lovely food in the English Market. St Finbarr's Cathedral is fantastic. Went to see the old city jail today. Going to Fota Wildlife Park tomorrow.
Mary.

Were you able to guess which city the postcards were sent from?

CHECK-UP

1. From which city was postcard 1 sent?
2. In what city is the house of Anne Frank?
3. Where would you hear Big Ben's bells ringing?
4. In what city would you find the English Market?
5. Outside which city would you find the pyramids?

Summer Camp

☆ **Soccer**
Swimming ☆
☆ **Sailing**
Hiking ☆
☆ **Hockey**
Horse Riding ☆

THE SUPER SUMMER CAMP!

☆ **Painting**
Pottery ☆
☆ **Picnics**
Cooking ☆
☆ **Camping**
Climbing ☆

Dates:
Mon 6th of July – Fri 10th of July
Mon 13th of July – Fri 17th of July
Mon 20th of July – Fri 24th of July

Times:
9am to 4pm daily

Ages:
Activities suitable for 6 to 10 year olds.

Prices:
One week: 50 euro
Two weeks: 90 euro
Three weeks: 130 euro

Family Discounts!

Please bring swimming togs, a pair of boots and a change of clothes each day.

Lunch will be provided.

Surname: _____
First name: _____
Age: _____
Address: _____
_____
_____

Parent's phone no.:
Home _____
Mob. _____
Work _____

Payment by (tick box):
Credit card ☐
Cheque ☐
Cash ☐

I wish to enrol in THE SUPER SUMMER CAMP for (tick box):
Week 1 ☐
Week 2 ☐
Week 3 ☐

CHECK-UP
1. What is the name of the camp?
2. For how many weeks does it run?
3. What age group is the camp suitable for?
4. What craft activity can you do in the camp?
5. Why do you think it is cheaper to go for more than one week?

Henry VIII

Henry VIII was born in 1491. He was crowned King of England when he was just 17 years old. Henry loved hunting, music, feasting and fine clothes. At first, everyone was very happy that he was king.

Soon after he became king, he married **Catherine of Aragon**, who was Spanish. Although they were married for 23 years, they had only one child, a girl called Mary. Henry VIII was not happy about this because he wanted a son. In those days, most people thought that only boys were good at ruling countries. Henry decided to divorce Catherine. He then married **Anne Boleyn**.

Anne was young and pretty. Henry was happy to be married to her. That year, Anne had a baby girl. They called her Elizabeth. Anne then had two more babies but very sadly they died. Henry was not happy at all as he still wanted to have a son. He decided to have Anne's head chopped off!

Henry then married his third wife. Her name was **Jane Seymour**. She had a baby boy named Edward. Sadly, Jane died a few days later.

Soon after Jane died, Henry got married again. His fourth wife was called **Anne of Cleves**. However, he did not like her at all and they divorced.

Henry's fifth wife was **Catherine Howard**. Henry didn't like her and her head was chopped off too!

By now Henry was getting old and very fat. He decided to get married for a sixth time, this time to **Catherine Parr**. They were only married for three years when Henry died in 1547.

After Henry VIII died, his son Edward became the new king.

CHECK-UP

1 What age was Henry when he became King of England?
2 Who was his first wife?
3 Where did she come from?
4 Which of Henry's wives had a baby boy?
5 Who became King of England after Henry died?

The New Girl

A new girl came to our class today. She had long dark hair and big green eyes. Teacher put her sitting beside me.

'My name is Zarabella,' she told us.

'Zara what?' shouted big Tom Diggins, the class bully. 'Zara who? That's a stupid name!' he laughed.

'That's alright,' said Zarabella sweetly. 'Even a fool like you will be able to say my name if you try really hard.'

We all laughed but Tom Diggins didn't. He went red in the face.

When we went out to the yard to play, Tom pushed Zarabella over onto the ground. She got up and looked at him with her big green eyes.

'Why don't you go for a big, long walk?' she said quietly. She wiggled her ears. Then Tom Diggins started to walk around the yard. He couldn't stop. He just kept walking, faster and faster.

He zoomed around for the whole break.

'I can't stop!' he wailed.

He only stopped when the bell rang. By then, he was pretty tired and very quiet. He didn't look at Zarabella as he limped back to class. Zarabella smiled.

'How did you do that?' I asked her.

'Oh, it's easy,' she grinned, 'when you can do magic tricks!' ■

CHECK-UP

1. What was the new girl's name?
2. Who was the class bully?
3. What did he do to Zarabella at break time?
4. What did Zarabella do then?
5. What did she wiggle?

Shark!

There are about 400 different kinds of shark in the world. Sharks are very good hunters. They can smell and sense other fish swimming more than one kilometre away. Many sharks are also very fast swimmers.

Some sharks can be found in the waters around Ireland. These include blue sharks, basking sharks and dogfish.

Not all sharks have big, sharp teeth. In fact, the two biggest sharks in the world have lots of tiny teeth. The whale shark is the world's biggest fish and the basking shark is the second biggest. They feed by swimming along, scooping up big mouthfuls of tiny sea creatures called **plankton**. They are very gentle sharks. They are very different to the great white shark and the bull shark, which are very fierce. The great white shark and the bull shark will attack the largest fish and even seals. Sometimes, they mistake people in the water for seals and attack them. The good news is that these sharks do not usually live near Ireland!

CHECK-UP

1. About how many kinds of shark are there in the world?
2. From how far away can a shark sense other fish?
3. Name some sharks that can be found near Ireland.
4. What do whale sharks eat?
5. Why do some sharks attack people?

A Recycling Song For Your School

(Sing this song to the tune of 'Mud, Mud, Glorious Mud'.)

Green, Green

We'll recycle batteries
and old bottle tops
with cardboard and paper each day.
We'll gather the packaging that
comes from the shops
and put it all safely away.
All those fruit skins will stay out of the bins,
we'll compost the whole lot instead.
It's all quite a bargain,
and good for the garden.
We really should all use our heads.

Green, green, it's time to think green.
Let's all save the planet,
the waste is obscene.
So pick up those papers,
do recycling capers,
our whole school is going to
keep the world green.

CHECK-UP

1. What is this song about?
2. Make a list of the things in the song that can be recycled.
3. What can you do with fruit skins?
4. Why is this good for the garden?
5. Do you think you can sing this song? Try it!

Marco Polo

Marco Polo lived in Venice in Italy about 700 years ago. When he was a teenager, he went with his father and uncle on a long, long journey to China.

In those days, there were no aeroplanes or cars. The roads were not very good either. They travelled through mountains and deserts, sometimes walking and sometimes riding on mules or horses.

They travelled for many, many months. They must have seen some amazing things on the way. However, the most amazing land of all was China. The people of China had many clever things that Marco had never seen before. They knew how to print books. They had clothes made of silk. They even had gunpowder that they used to make fireworks.

Marco, his father and uncle went to the palace of the Emperor of China. They stayed there for many years. They told the Emperor about Italy and learned all about China from him.

They stayed away from home for about 24 years! At last, they left China and went back to Venice. This time, they sailed most of the way. However, they still had to travel some parts of the journey over land.

When Marco got home, he wrote a book about all the amazing things he had seen. The book was very popular. It made lots of other people want to go to China too.

CHECK-UP

1. In what Italian city did Marco Polo live?
2. Who did he go travelling with?
3. What amazing new things did they find there?
4. How long did they spend in China?
5. What did Marco do when he got home?

Love and Hate

Lucy hated going to her bed at night, but she loved her bed in the morning. Every night, there was 'war' in Lucy's house because she would not go to bed when she was told. Every morning, there was 'war' in Lucy's house because she would not get up when she was told!

So her parents took her to see Dr Daft. Lucy sat on a big seat in Dr Daft's office. He took out an old watch on a chain.

'Look at my watch, Lucy,' he said. He then slowly swung the watch in front of Lucy's eyes. Soon she began to feel sleepy.

'From now on, you will love the things that you hate and hate the things that you love,' said Dr Daft.

Dr Daft's cure worked! Now Lucy loves her bed at night and hates it in the morning! There is no more 'war' at home! It is not just bedtime that has changed in Lucy's house. Lucy used to love watching TV and hate reading. But now she hates watching TV and her head is always in a book! She used to love sweets and hate vegetables. Now she won't touch a sweet but she can't get enough broccoli!

Lucy's life has changed … but not all for the better. She used to love looking clean and tidy. But now she is a complete mess! ■

CHECK-UP
1. What is the title of the story?
2. What is the girl's name?
3. Why was there 'war' in her house every night and every morning?
4. What vegetable does she like now?
5. Have all the changes in her life been good? Explain your answer.

CATS

Pet cats have big dangerous cousins. These cousins are not the sort of cats that purr when you rub their tummies. They live in the wild and humans should never get too close to them.

Lions, tigers, cheetahs, jaguars and leopards are all members of the cat family. They are strong, fast and fierce animals. They are **carnivores** (meat eaters) and have sharp teeth and claws.

The lion is the king of the African cats. Lions live in **prides**. A pride is a family group of about 12 lions. There are usually two male lions in a pride. The female lionesses and baby cubs make up the rest of the pride. The powerful male lion has a thick mane of fur around his neck and chest. The male lions protect the pride. The lionesses raise the cubs.

Tigers are found in forests, mainly in India and Sumatra. This magnificent big cat has black stripes on its brown coat. These help keep the tiger hidden while it sneaks up on its prey deep in the forest. When it catches a deer or a wild pig, the tiger will drag it away to a quiet place to eat. Tigers and jaguars are the only wild cats that enjoy being in water.

Leopards live in Africa and Asia. They usually have a spotted coat. Panthers are black leopards but they do not have spots. Leopards are very good at climbing trees and hide their food in the branches. Jaguars look like leopards but their spots are larger. Jaguars live in the forests of South America. These are just some of the pet cat's wilder relatives.

CHECK-UP

1. Name four cousins of the pet cat.
2. What is a carnivore?
3. Where do lions live?
4. What is a family of lions called?
5. Which wild cats like the water?

Mice

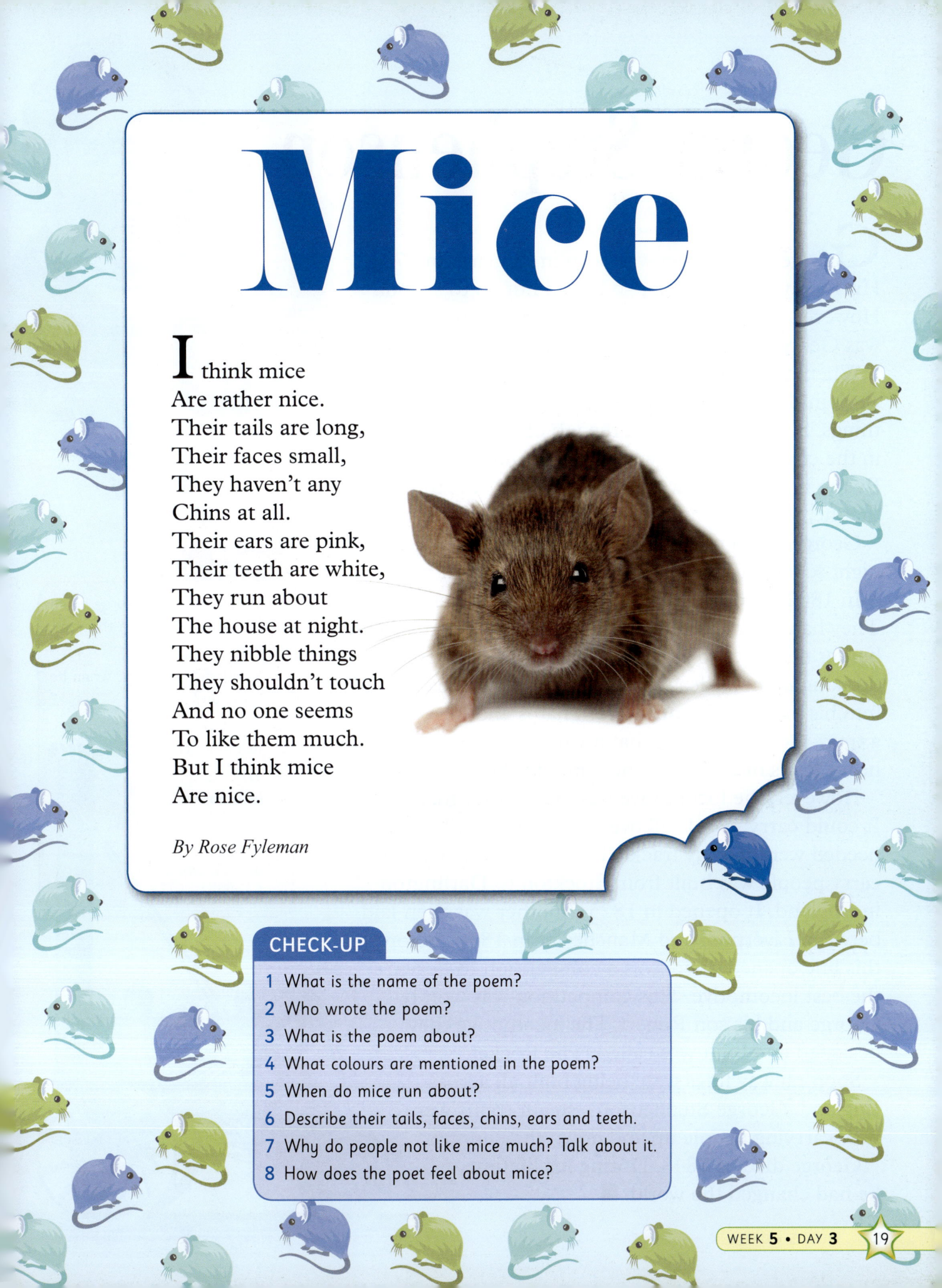

I think mice
Are rather nice.
Their tails are long,
Their faces small,
They haven't any
Chins at all.
Their ears are pink,
Their teeth are white,
They run about
The house at night.
They nibble things
They shouldn't touch
And no one seems
To like them much.
But I think mice
Are nice.

By Rose Fyleman

CHECK-UP

1. What is the name of the poem?
2. Who wrote the poem?
3. What is the poem about?
4. What colours are mentioned in the poem?
5. When do mice run about?
6. Describe their tails, faces, chins, ears and teeth.
7. Why do people not like mice much? Talk about it.
8. How does the poet feel about mice?

George Stephenson

George Stephenson was born in England in 1781. His family was very poor so he did not go to school. However, George had a wonderful mind. In fact, it was George who invented the steam engine.

When he was a young teenager, George went to work in the coal mines with his father. He loved fixing things. Soon, he was given the job of fixing machines in the coal mine. The owners of the mine were pleased. By the time George was 17 years of age, it is thought that he was his own father's boss!

George could not read or write so he started going to night school after work. He was really good at maths.

In 1802, George got married to Frances Henderson. They had a son called Robert. George now had to work harder than ever to support his family. He never stopped thinking up new ideas. One day, a brilliant idea flashed into his mind – a **locomotive**! That is another word for a train. George thought that it would be great for pulling heavy loads of coal from the mines to the factories.

However, the locomotive was even better than that. It could carry people all over the country. All that was needed were railway tracks. The first railway track to carry people was built from Stockton to Darlington in England. It opened in 1825. Another was then laid between Liverpool and Manchester in 1830. Before this line opened, there was a competition to design the best locomotive. This competition was won by George and his son Robert. The locomotive they designed and built was called 'The Rocket'.

Soon railway lines were being built all across England. George Stephenson's steam trains were now carrying people up and down the country.

George died in 1848. During his lifetime, he had changed the world. ■

CHECK-UP

1. What age was George when he went to work in the coal mines?
2. What did he invent when he grew up?
3. What was his best subject at night school?
4. What is a locomotive?
5. George was born in 1781. What age was he when he died?

The Sea Cave

We were on holiday in Wexford. We had gone to a beach that Dad knew well. Rocky cliffs rose up around it and waves lapped up on its golden sand. We were the only people there. I ran along the wet sand near the cliffs as Mam and Dad walked behind me. That's when I chanced to see what I thought was a cave.

It was a big, black hole in the cliff, like a giant's mouth trying to eat the sand.

'Look what I found!' I called out. 'Can we go inside?'

Mam and Dad arrived at the cave and I followed them inside. There was barely enough light to see. There were shells and bits of seaweed on the wet sandy floor. The roof got lower as we went further inside. We walked for about a minute, until we could go no further.

'This is cool!' I said.

We were just about to leave the cave when I saw a half-buried bottle. I pulled it out of the wet sand. There was something inside. A letter!

Dad took the top off the bottle. I pulled the letter out carefully. We read what it said. ■

CHECK-UP

1 Where was the family on holiday?
2 What was the first thing the child found?
3 Who opened the bottle?
4 From where had the letter been sent?
5 How do you think the bottle got into the cave?

Greetings from America! If you find this letter, please write back to:
Alvin Bloomberg,
1187 Franklin Street,
Miami, Florida, USA.

Blue Planet

Earth is called the Blue Planet because about two-thirds of its surface is covered by water. Most of this is salt water. The water around the shores of Ireland is about 100–150 metres deep. However, it gets much deeper as you move out into the Atlantic Ocean. The bottom of the Atlantic Ocean is about four kilometres below the surface. This is too deep for sunlight to reach. Many strange sea creatures live there. The deepest water in the world is a massive 11 kilometres below the surface. It is so deep that nobody has ever gone to the bottom, not even in a submarine.

Many of the world's animals and plants live in the seas and oceans. Some are so tiny you would need a microscope to see them. They are called **plankton**. There are many more kinds of fish than there are birds or land mammals. The seas and oceans are home to more than just fish. Seals, whales and dolphins are all mammals that live in these waters. Many new kinds of sea animals are discovered every year. Many more are still to be found. Amazingly, we know more about outer space than we do about the seas and oceans of our own planet.

CHECK-UP

1. Why is Earth called the Blue Planet?
2. How deep is the water around the shores of Ireland?
3. How deep is the deepest water in the world?
4. What are plankton?
5. Are there more fish than birds in the world?

LOST!
A Much-Loved Family Pet

- Fluffy is a three-year-old male gorilla. He was last seen playing in the trees in the park. He escaped from his steel cage in our back garden on Tuesday morning. (The park keeper hopes to have all the trees planted again soon. Sorry about that.)

- Fluffy has thick black fur. He is about 1.5 metres tall when he stands up on his legs. However, he only does this when he wants to scare people off. That only happens sometimes. Fluffy is normally very friendly and playful. He can be a little rough, however, so don't try to pet him or anything like that. You might frighten him.

- He is very fond of cars. He has a little trick of ripping their bumpers off and tying them in knots. He also likes bicycles and will sometimes take the wheels off just for fun. He is just full of fun!

- If you see Fluffy playing with a car, a bicycle or a lamp-post outside your house, please call the number below. We will come and collect him straight away. It's also probably best if you don't go too near him.

Reward offered

Phone number: 089-1005889722

CHECK-UP

1. What kind of animal has been lost?
2. What is his name?
3. What happened to the trees in the park?
4. What little tricks does he like to get up to?
5. Why is it not a good idea to get too close to Fluffy?

THE Spirit of Saint Louis

Charles Lindbergh was an American pilot. His job was to fly across America carrying letters for the Post Office. However, his dream was to become the first person to fly across the Atlantic Ocean alone.

Charles had a special aeroplane built that could carry lots of fuel for the long journey. He called his aeroplane the *Spirit of Saint Louis* after the town where he lived. It was a very dangerous journey. Six people had already died trying the same flight. On the 20th of May 1927, he took off from New York. He headed out across the vast Atlantic Ocean. He was all alone, just him and his aeroplane.

It was a very scary flight. He had to fly through thick fog and lashing rain. Sometimes he went too high and it got icy. Sometimes he went too low and nearly hit the ocean! He had to stay awake for a very long time. He ate only one sandwich and drank some water to keep himself going.

The first land he saw, after he had crossed the Atlantic Ocean, was Dingle in County Kerry. It cheered him up a lot but he did not land there. His target was Paris in France.

After nearly 34 hours, he saw the bright lights of Paris. He landed at an airport there. He had done it. He was the first person to fly alone across the Atlantic Ocean. He was famous!

CHECK-UP

1. Where was Charles Lindbergh from?
2. What was his job?
3. What was the name of his aeroplane?
4. How long did the flight take?
5. Where did he land after the flight?

999

This is the emergency operator. Which service do you need?

Em. Look ... I ... it's a fire. I need a fire brigade!

Please stay calm and I'll get help to you quickly. What is your phone number?

Look, there's a house on fire! You need to ...

Please tell me where you are ringing from so that I can ring you back if I need to.

Oh. I'm ringing from a call box in Hill Street.

Where is that? Can you give me the number of the phone?

I'm in Ballymore and the number is 09768 357427177.

And what is your name?

Jack Dunne, you need to ...

Where is the fire, Jack?

It's a house in Hill Street. There is smoke pouring out of one of the upstairs windows.

Is there anyone in the house?

I don't know but I do know that an old man lives there.

I have alerted the fire brigade and will also send an ambulance. Can you stay near that phone until they arrive or are you in any danger from the fire if you stay there?

No. I'm fine. I'll stay here till they come.

Thank you. Help should be there in about four minutes.

Thanks.

CHECK-UP

1. To whom was the young boy talking?
2. Where was the fire?
3. Where was the boy making the phone call from?
4. What was the boy's name?
5. Who lived in the house?

CARS

The first 'car' was made by a Frenchman called Nicolas Cugnot in 1769. This 'car' ran on steam. It was used by the French army to pull heavy cannons!

In the olden days, cars were not allowed to be driven faster than a person walking. A man carrying a red flag had to walk in front of the car to warn people that it was coming. These cars were called *horseless carriages*.

In 1886, two German engineers named Karl Benz and Gottlieb Daimler invented cars with engines. These cars ran quite like the cars we have nowadays.

In 1903, Henry Ford set up the Ford Motor Company in America. In 1908, the Ford Motor Company made a car called the Ford Model T. The company made millions of these cheaper cars. People could now afford to buy them. These cars were very popular all over the world.

In the early days, only very rich people had cars. Nowadays, many people have cars. Cars are getting better all of the time. They are safer and cleaner than they used to be. This is better for our world. I wonder what sort of car you will be driving when you grow up. ■

CHECK-UP

1. Who made the first 'car'?
2. Who had to walk in front of cars in the early days? Why?
3. What were these first cars called?
4. In what year was the Ford Motor Company set up?
5. Why was the Ford Model T car so popular?

Recipe: Buns

For this recipe, you need:

1. A bun tin
2. A mixing bowl
3. A sieve
4. Paper bun cases
5. A wooden spoon
6. A cereal spoon

Ingredients:

2 eggs
100g soft margarine
100g self-raising flour
100g caster sugar

Instructions:

1. Pre-heat the oven to 180°C (gas mark 4). Ask an adult to help you.
2. Put the paper bun cases in the bun tin.
3. Sieve the flour into the mixing bowl.
4. Add the caster sugar and the margarine.
5. Break the eggs into the mixing bowl.
6. Stir all the ingredients together until the mixture is smooth.
7. Put a cereal spoonful of the mixture into each paper bun case.
8. Ask an adult to bake the buns in the oven for 10 to 15 minutes. They will be golden brown when cooked.
9. Let the buns cool before eating them!

Note: You might like to decorate your buns with chocolate, Smarties or icing sugar before serving them.

CHECK-UP

1. What do you use the sieve for?
2. How hot should the oven be?
3. What weight of margarine do you use in the recipe?
4. How many eggs are needed?
5. How long do the buns take to bake?
6. What suggestions are made for decorating the buns?
7. How would you decorate the buns?

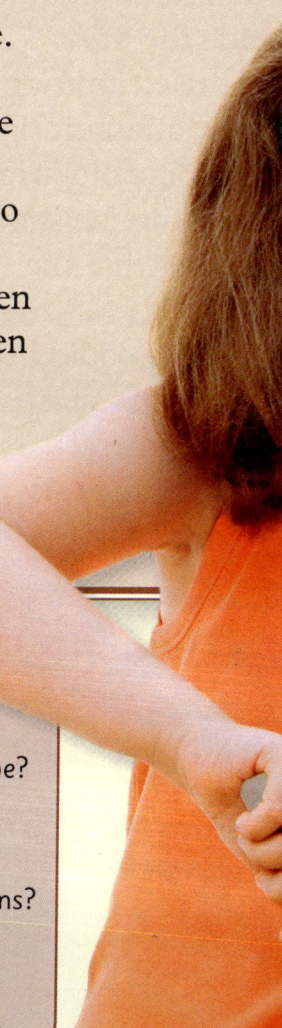

John Logie Baird

We all watch it but not many people know who invented television. This inventor's name was John Logie Baird. He was born in 1888 in Scotland. Even as a small boy, he loved inventing things. Using wires and tin cans, he once linked up all the houses on his street with 'telephones'. However, the wires hanging across the road caused a horse and carriage to have an accident. John had to take the wires down. He did not mind though. He put the wires to good use and made electric lights for his house.

When he grew up, John Logie Baird moved to London to work. Even though he was very poor, he kept inventing things out of ordinary materials that he could find anywhere.

That is how he made the first television in 1926. He used knitting needles, a bicycle lamp, a biscuit tin, wires, old motors and some old army equipment. The first picture he showed on his '**televisor**' (that is what the first televisions were called) was of a ventriloquist's dummy. He could not find anyone brave enough to sit in front of his homemade camera!

Next time you are watching television, remember John Logie Baird. We have a lot to thank him for! ■

CHECK-UP

1 Who invented television?
2 In what year was he born?
3 Where did he move to when he grew up?
4 What did he make his television out of?
5 Why do you think people were afraid to sit in front of his camera?

In the Woods

Aunt Dora brought us for an evening walk in the woods beside her house. The autumn evening sunlight streamed through the branches as we passed the first trees. The leaves above us glowed green and yellow as they caught the light. Dead leaves covered the ground in a deep blanket of red, brown and gold.

We could hear the stream before we saw it. The water made a tinkling and gurgling sound as it flowed over the smooth round rocks. Dora said that the water was safe to drink. I dipped my hand in to scoop some up. The water was crystal clear and icy cold. It tasted great.

A squirrel jumped from one branch of a tree to another over our heads. The woods were full of squirrels, badgers, mice and hedgehogs. There were owls and foxes too.

I stopped to pick up a small feather. It was an amazing shade of bright blue with black stripes. Dora said it was from a jay.

I wanted to pick the red toadstools when I saw them. They looked just like something out of a fairy tale.

'Don't touch them Jim,' said Dora. 'They are poisonous and could make you very sick. Or worse! Come on. We'll head back. It's time for tea.'

CHECK-UP

1 What was the aunt's name?
2 List all the colours mentioned in the story.
3 What was the water in the stream like?
4 Name all the animals mentioned in the story.
5 Why did Dora not let him pick the toadstool?

Nuts and Seeds

All plants need sunlight to grow, from the smallest moss to the biggest tree. They do not grow well in the winter because it is too dark and cold. Things begin to happen when spring starts. Buds grow into leaves. Flowers start to bloom. Seeds in the ground start to grow into plants.

The summer is the best time for plants. This is when they make their seeds. They use the light from the sun all summer long. Some trees make big seeds, or nuts, such as chestnuts.

By the time autumn comes, the seeds and nuts have grown. They fall off the tree or the plant onto the ground. They will wait all through the winter before they start to grow in the next spring. Not all seeds and nuts have a chance to grow. People and animals use seeds and nuts for food. For example, squirrels gather acorns and hazelnuts and store them for winter. People gather lots of seeds for food too. Peas, beans, rice and corn are all seeds that we eat. Wheat seeds are turned into flour to make cakes and bread. Animals get their seeds from wild plants but people get them mostly from farms.

CHECK-UP

1. Do plants grow well in the winter? Why is that?
2. When do plants grow best?
3. When are seeds and nuts fully grown?
4. Name some seeds that people eat.
5. From where do people get most of their seeds?

HALLOWE'EN SHOPPING LIST

One jar of frogs' eyes
Two dragons' teeth
A packet of crows' feathers
Wart cream
Ten lizards' tails
Three dead men's skulls (medium size)
Half a kilo of dried poisonous mushrooms
Large sack of dried nettles
Snake venom (whatever kind they have in the shop)
Two packets of dried spiders
One bag of fresh spiders
Two large bottles of tiger blood
Pipe tobacco
Large bag of dandelion roots
Four dried jellyfish (with stingers left on)
Small bucket of frogspawn
Bottle of toad juice
Teabags
Sugar
Small tub of powdered unicorn horn
Hello! magazine
Green lipstick
Two bags of dead men's fingernails
Fish fingers
Frozen chips

CHECK-UP

1. Name all the animals on the list.
2. Which of the animals are make-believe ones?
3. How many dried things can you find on the list?
4. Are there any poisonous things on the list? Name them.
5. Are there any things that you might find on a normal shopping list? Name them.

Alice the Witch of Kilkenny

Alice Kyteler (*Kit-ler*) was born in Kilkenny about 700 years ago. She must have been very nice because she got married quite a lot. Four times in fact! The interesting thing is that all of her husbands died when they were quite young. Nobody ever knew exactly what had killed them.

People began to think there was something a bit strange about Alice. Maybe she was just a bit unlucky, falling in love with a load of unhealthy men with bad coughs. Or maybe it was something else.

Each of Alice's four husbands had given her money and she had become very wealthy. Some of her family were a bit jealous and claimed that she was a witch. They said she had all sorts of bottles and strange mixtures hidden in a box in her room. She just had to be a witch! That's what everybody else said.

In those days, anyone thought to be a witch was in **big** trouble. The local bishop decided to have Alice arrested and put on trial. However, Alice found out about this. She decided to flee to England. Nobody in Kilkenny ever heard of her again.

Was Alice a witch or was it just jealous people spreading rumours? We will never know for sure.

CHECK-UP

1 Where did Alice live?
2 How many times was she married?
3 Was Alice rich or poor?
4 What did some of her family say about her?
5 Who wanted to arrest her?

The Guitar Man

When the *Our Town Has Talent* contest came to town, Simon was the first one to enter. The winner would go on to the *All-Ireland Talent Show*.

That night, the hall was packed. Simon was introduced as 'The Guitar Man'.

'Oh no,' moaned Mum. 'He doesn't even have a guitar.'

'Play this … as loudly as you can!' Simon told the sound man. He handed him a CD.

Suddenly, the hall filled with rock music. Simon started plucking at his air guitar. Everyone laughed, but Simon was deadly serious. He whirled his right arm around like a windmill. The fingers of his left hand raced up and down the imaginary neck of his air guitar. The music was pumping from the speakers.

As the music got faster, Simon started shaking his head. Then he slid to the front of the stage on his knees. He played his air guitar over his head and behind his back. Soon, the members of the audience were on their feet. They too were plucking away at air guitars and shaking their hair all over their faces.

When the music ended, there was a huge cheer. Simon flung his air guitar into the crowd!

Guess who was going to the *All-Ireland Talent Show* from our town? ■

CHECK-UP

1. What was the name of the local contest?
2. Who was the first person to enter the contest?
3. What did Simon give the sound man?
4. How did the audience react at first?
5. What did Simon do with his air guitar at the end of his song?

Under Your Feet!

We walk around on top of the ground. We see dogs, cats, cows and birds all living on top of the ground like we do. However, there are lots of other animals living in the dark, under the ground.

Moles build tunnels under the ground with their strong front paws. They like to eat worms and insect eggs. Moles cannot see very well. However, they do not need sight in their dark world. There are no moles in Ireland. In countries where they do live, you can see little hills of soil in gardens as they dig, looking for food.

Earthworms also live under the ground. Gardeners like them because they break up the soil as they move through it. This allows air and rain to reach the roots of plants, making it easier for them to grow. An earthworm is like a tube. It swallows soil, which passes right through it as it moves along.

Under your feet, there are probably hundreds of ants hurrying around, busy in their underground nests.

Animals like foxes, badgers, mice and rabbits also live under the ground. They build their holes, burrows, dens or tunnels beneath the earth. They usually only come out to feed at night.

As you can see, there is a lot going on under your feet!

CHECK-UP

1. What animals might we see when we walk around?
2. Are there any moles in Ireland?
3. Why do gardeners like earthworms?
4. Name an insect that might be under your feet right now.
5. Do badgers, rabbits and foxes stay underground all of the time?

Polar Bears

Polar bears are the largest of all bears. They live on the ice that covers the Arctic Circle at the top of the world. They mostly eat seals. A polar bear will wait quietly at a seal's breathing hole in the ice. When the seal pops its head out of the hole, the polar bear moves fast. It grabs the seal with its sharp, jagged teeth.

Sometimes, a polar bear creeps up on a seal resting on the ice. The bear's beautiful white coat makes it hard to see against the white snow and ice. When the seal finally spots the bear, it is usually too late. The polar bear will charge and catch the seal with its powerful claws before it can escape. Polar bears are good swimmers. They often hunt below the ice.

In the autumn, the female polar bear makes a den in a snowdrift. During the long winter, she gives birth to one or two baby bears called **cubs**. In the spring, the mother comes out of her den with her young cubs. She nurses them for about two years. She teaches them how to hunt and protect themselves.

Polar bears are beautiful animals. They are in danger of extinction because the ice around the Arctic Circle is melting. Some scientists say there will be no more polar bears in the wild within 100 years if global warming is not stopped. ■

CHECK-UP

1. Where do polar bears live?
2. What does the female polar bear do in the autumn?
3. How many cubs does a female bear give birth to?
4. How long does she nurse the cubs for?
5. What are polar bears in danger of?

Louis Braille

Louis Braille was born in a French village in 1809. His father made saddles for horses. One day, when Louis was three years old, he climbed up onto a stool in his father's workshop. He took a sharp knife and tried to cut some leather. The stool slipped and Louis cut his eye with the knife. His eye became infected. The infection then spread to his other eye and Louis became blind.

Louis now had to learn everything through touching and hearing.

When he was 10 years old, Louis went to a special school for blind children in Paris. There, he learned how to make baskets and slippers. He also learned how to play the piano and became very good at it. He loved history and maths but he could not read or write.

One day, an old soldier came to visit the school. He taught the students a secret code that the army used. It was called 'night-writing'. It used dashes and dots punched into paper instead of letters. Louis could read 'night-writing' with his fingers by touching the pushed-up dashes and dots on the paper. However, Louis found it quite difficult. He decided to come up with an easier system. He invented Braille. This system used only six raised dots for the whole alphabet. By touching the dots, a blind person could read.

What a breakthrough. Nowadays, blind people all over the world read Braille books and write with Braille computers.

Louis died when he was 43 years old. Thanks to his important invention, his name will never be forgotten. ■

CHECK-UP

1 What country was Louis Braille from?
2 What was his father's job?
3 Why could Louis not read or write?
4 Where did he go to school when he was 10 years old?
5 What is the name of the reading system that Louis invented?

A Letter to Say Sorry

17 Fairytale Drive,
Fairytown,
Fairyland.

21 February

Dear Mr and Mrs Bear,

   I would like to say how sorry I am for all the trouble I caused you. I don't know what came over me. I am normally a very good girl. I think it was the lovely smell of porridge coming from your house that made me do it. Maybe I was a little bit hungry too. One minute, I was walking along the path being as good as good can be. Then, before I could stop myself, I was climbing through your window. I know this was wrong. I am really very sorry.

   I am not blaming you but I did burn my tongue quite badly with that first spoonful of porridge. It was also very greedy of me to eat all of Baby Bear's porridge. I promise to stick to cornflakes from now on.

   I am also very sorry about the chair I broke. I am saving up my pocket money to buy a new one for Baby Bear. Please forgive me. I hope we can all be friends some day.

Yours sincerely,
Goldilocks

PS. I hope the muddy footprints I left on your bed sheets came out in the wash.

CHECK-UP

1. Who wrote this letter?
2. Who is she writing to?
3. What did she do to her tongue?
4. What did she break?
5. How does she plan to buy a new chair?

Squirrels

Cute and furry with lovely bushy tails, everyone likes squirrels. It does not seem to matter that they are cousins of mice and rats. People still like them. Squirrels live in woods and forests. They eat nuts and seeds that they get from trees. They collect nuts in the autumn and store them for times when food is scarce.

Squirrels can jump quickly from branch to branch high up in the trees. This keeps them safe from **predators** such as foxes. They come down from the trees when they want to hide some nuts in the ground and to look for more food.

There are two kinds of squirrel in Ireland – the red squirrel and the grey squirrel. Red squirrels have been in Ireland for thousands of years. Grey squirrels only arrived in Ireland about 100 years ago. In 1911, a few grey squirrels were brought over from America as a wedding present for an important lady. They escaped and went into the wild. Nowadays, there are more grey squirrels in Ireland than red ones.

In the winter, squirrels sleep a lot. They live in special nests called **dreys**. When they wake up feeling hungry, they go looking for the nuts that they have stored.

CHECK-UP

1. In what areas do squirrels like to live?
2. Why do they spend so much time up in trees?
3. What do they eat?
4. How many kinds of squirrel live in Ireland?
5. What is the nest of a squirrel called?

Look at the Picture

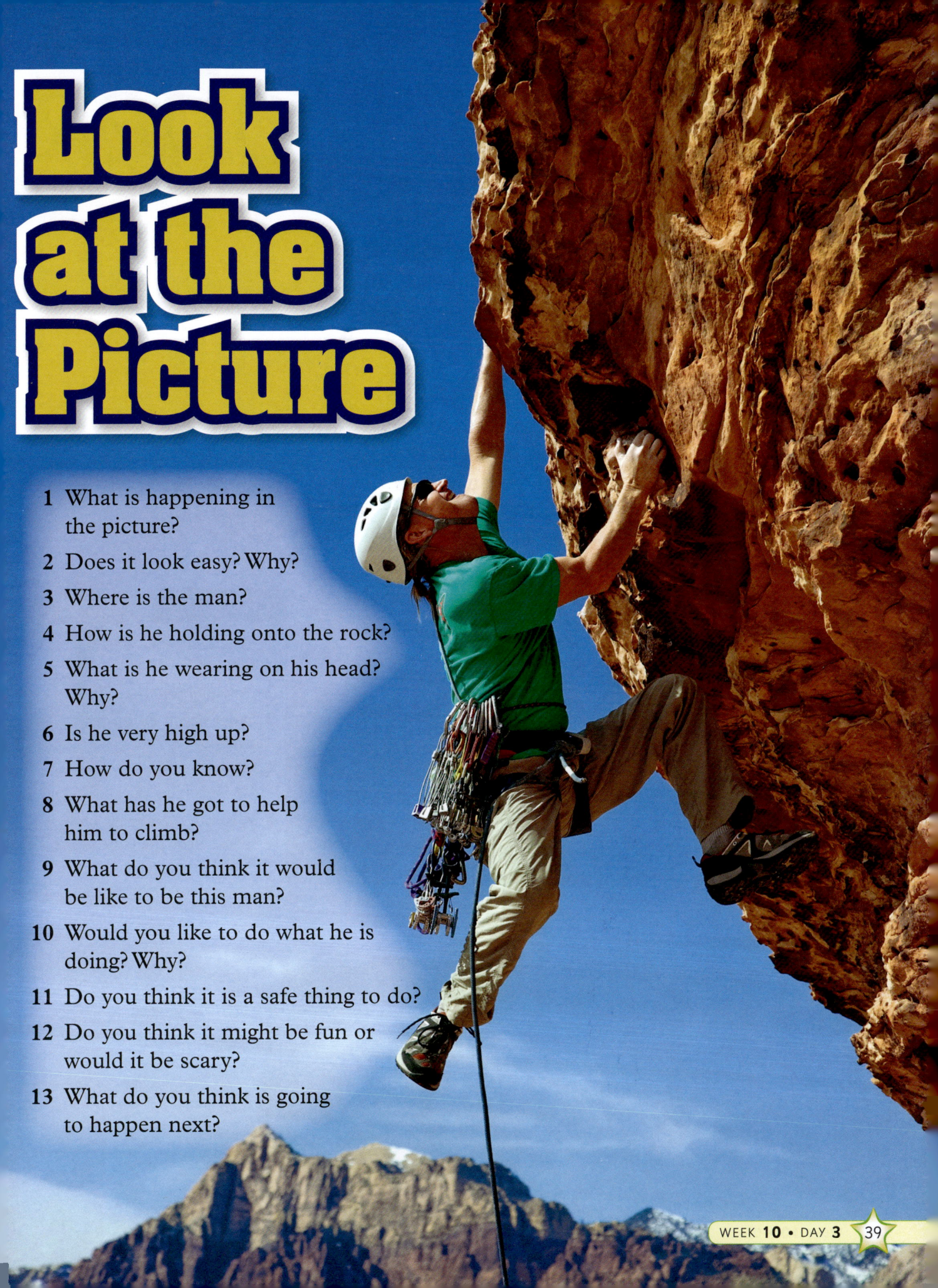

1. What is happening in the picture?
2. Does it look easy? Why?
3. Where is the man?
4. How is he holding onto the rock?
5. What is he wearing on his head? Why?
6. Is he very high up?
7. How do you know?
8. What has he got to help him to climb?
9. What do you think it would be like to be this man?
10. Would you like to do what he is doing? Why?
11. Do you think it is a safe thing to do?
12. Do you think it might be fun or would it be scary?
13. What do you think is going to happen next?

Cliffs of Moher

The Cliffs of Moher are in County Clare. They are among the highest cliffs in Ireland. They rise 214 metres from the Atlantic Ocean. Stretching for eight kilometres along the coast, the cliffs are one of Ireland's most famous beauty spots.

Great rolling waves from the Atlantic Ocean crash against the base of the cliffs. The ocean below them is nearly always white with foam and froth. The waves are often huge. However, they can seem tiny against the mighty wall of rock. Over many years, the ocean has eaten away parts of the cliffs, making sea caves and arches.

The rock in the cliffs is **sandstone** and **black shale**. The rock was formed over millions of years. Layers of mud and sand built up and were squeezed together. They turned to stone.

The cliffs are home to many seabirds that make their nests there. You can see the birds flying over the ocean and diving into it, looking for fish.

Thousands of people visit the cliffs every day. There is a special visitors' centre to help people find out more about the cliffs. There are also walls and fences to stop people going too near the edge of the cliffs. This is important as it is a very long way down to the ocean!

CHECK-UP

1 Where are the Cliffs of Moher?
2 How high are the cliffs?
3 What ocean do the cliffs overlook?
4 What special place is there for visitors to the cliffs?
5 Why are there walls and fences near the edge of the cliffs?

Pocket Genie

In my Christmas cracker, I got a paper hat, a silly joke and a tiny, red plastic bottle. I unscrewed the tiny lid of the bottle. A tiny genie popped out with a tiny puff of smoke! He wore a turban on his head.

'I am a pocket genie,' he declared, sitting cross-legged in mid-air. 'Your wish is my command, oh mistress.'

I asked for three wishes but, sadly, pocket genies don't do wishes. However, they do a lot of other things.

When I go to my bedroom to do my homework, I open the tiny, red bottle. Out pops pocket genie and with a nod of his head my homework is all done. Perfectly! My teacher calls me Lady Einstein.

I used to hate chores. Now, I ask if I can empty the dishwasher, make the beds, tidy up, weed the garden and wash the car. All I have to do is unscrew the bottle and …

'Your wish is my command, oh mistress,' says pocket genie. With a nod of his head, the job is done. My parents call me Mary Poppins!

Pocket genie is my secret. However, he has a brother hidden in a Christmas cracker. You could be lucky enough to find him!

CHECK-UP

1. What three things were in the Christmas cracker?
2. Why was the genie called a 'pocket' genie?
3. What did he call the girl who opened the bottle?
4. Why does the girl's teacher call her Lady Einstein?
5. What do her parents call her? Why?

Sherpas

The Sherpa people live in a country called Nepal. It is beside Mount Everest, the highest mountain in the world. Mount Everest is 8,848 metres high. Sherpas live high up in mountain villages. There are no roads or cars. They hike everywhere, often carrying huge loads on their backs. To get to school, some Sherpa children have to hike up more than 300 metres. That is about 100 floors in a skyscraper.

The air at the top of Mount Everest is very thin. Climbers have to bring up their own oxygen tanks. The temperatures are freezing. The weather can change in an instant, making it the most dangerous climb in the world. The Sherpas are Mount Everest experts. They know if there is going to be a blizzard or an avalanche. Anyone who wants to climb Mount Everest has to bring lots of equipment. Therefore, they usually need to have Sherpas with them. Sherpas and their yaks help to carry the tents, food, drinks, ropes and hiking gear for the climbers. People rarely climb Mount Everest without a Sherpa guide.

The first man to climb to the top of Mount Everest was Sir Edmund Hillary. He was from New Zealand. His Sherpa guide was Tenzing Norgay. They reached the summit of the mountain on the 29th of May 1953.

Since 1953, many climbers have reached the summit of this huge mountain. It is agreed that few could have managed without the help of the Sherpas.

CHECK-UP

1 Nepal is on the slopes of what mountain?
2 Why do climbers usually have to bring oxygen tanks?
3 Why do climbers usually need Sherpa guides?
4 Who was the first man to reach the summit of Mount Everest?
5 What was the name of his Sherpa guide?

A Sense of Smell

Humans have five senses. They are sight, touch, hearing, taste and smell. Our sense of smell is one of the most important ones.

Our noses sense all the different smells that are in the air we breathe. There are tiny hairs inside our noses. These catch any dirt or dust that is in the air. There are lots of tiny nerves at the back of our noses. These sense different smells and send messages to the brain. Then the brain works out what the smell is.

Some smells are very pleasant. These smells (or scents) are often added to perfumes, soaps and even food to make us want to buy them. The taste of food is mixed up with its smell. Think of the lovely smell of strawberries or the sharp smell of vinegar. If food rots, it has a bad smell. Our brain tells us not to eat it.

Some people have to use their sense of smell in their job. For example, perfumers have an excellent sense of smell. Some can sense thousands of different smells! However, no matter how good their sense of smell is, they cannot smell as well as many animals.

Dogs have an amazing sense of smell. Because of this, they are often used to search for people after earthquakes. Sharks also have an amazing sense of smell. Not only can they smell a drop of blood in water from far away, they can even tell what direction the smell is coming from. No wonder they are so dangerous.

CHECK-UP

1. How are smells carried to our noses?
2. Why do we have tiny hairs in our noses?
3. Name (a) a sweet smell, (b) a sour smell and (c) your favourite smell.
4. How is a dog's amazing sense of smell sometimes used?
5. How does a shark's sense of smell help it to hunt?

Hans Christian Andersen

Hans Christian Andersen was a man who simply would not give up. He was born in 1805 in Odense in Denmark. His family was very poor. There was only one room in their house. Hans did not do well in school and some of the other children bullied him. When he was 14 years old, he went to Copenhagen to seek his fortune.

In Copenhagen, Hans tried singing, dancing and acting. He also wrote poems and plays. However, his efforts were not a success.

Hans would not give up. He went back to school. After six long and difficult years, he managed to pass all of his exams. However, people still would not read his books and plays. Everybody said, 'Give up, Hans. Find a proper job!'

Hans did not listen to them. One day, he started writing stories for children. Suddenly, he was a success. Everyone loved his fairy tales.

Hans published 156 fairy tales altogether. His most famous fairy tales are *The Little Mermaid*, *The Ugly Duckling*, *The Emperor's New Clothes* and *The Snow Queen*.

Hans became a rich man. He travelled all over Europe, staying with kings and queens. His own life was a fairy tale come true. When he died in 1875, the bells in Copenhagen were rung for him. ■

CHECK-UP

1. When was Hans Christian Andersen born?
2. Where was he born?
3. Where did he go to seek his fortune?
4. What were his most famous stories?
5. What did people in Copenhagen do when Hans died?

A Boat Trip

We only found out what was planned when Dad stopped the car. He pointed to the fishing boats tied up at the pier. The sign beside the pier said 'Boat Trips'.

'You're joking!' said Mam, giving Dad a funny look.

'It will be great!' he said as he led us to the boat.

We got on board the boat. The boatman gave us life jackets to wear. Dad took pictures of all of us in our life jackets. He was grinning broadly.

'This will be great!' he told us as the boat left the pier and headed out onto the sparkling, blue sea.

We felt the boat swaying gently as it moved along. The sea was like glass. There were hardly any waves. We sat back and enjoyed the blue sky, the blue sea and … Dad's green face.

He was seasick! In fact, he was *very* seasick.

'How long does the trip last?' he blurted at the boatman.

'Oh, about an hour,' the boatman said with a cheerful smile. 'The sea might get a bit choppy further out.'

'Oh,' said Dad.

Mam smiled and winked at us.

We all enjoyed the trip – well, everyone except Dad. He didn't say a word after we got off the boat back at the pier. ■

CHECK-UP

1. Whose idea was it to go on a boat trip?
2. Where were the boats?
3. What did everyone wear while they were on the boat?
4. Did Dad enjoy the trip?
5. List all the colours in the story.

Ring Ring

- Hello?
- Oh, Jack. How are you? … Sorry?
- Hang on. Slow down, you're talking nineteen to the dozen. I can hardly make out what you're saying. What's wrong?
- You're stuck where? On top of a phone box? What on earth are you doing there?
- What sheep? 
- Hold on. Let me get this straight. About 200 sheep are running loose in the main street of the village?
- But where did they come from?
- How on earth did they get out of the trailer in the first place?
- Yes, but what sort of twit would bump into the back door of a trailer carrying 200 sheep?
- Oh. Did anybody see you?
- Well, maybe they didn't notice in the panic. Maybe they'll think the door was faulty and you were just standing beside it when it opened. 
- Yes, well I'm not the twit who wasn't looking where he was going, am I? Anyway, what are the Gardaí doing about it?
- Really? The sheep are in the station as well? I suppose the Gardaí will be a bit busy then.
- Is anybody hurt?
- Well, that's something at least.
- Yes, I'll tell everybody that you're going to be a bit late. Right, see you later. 'Bye.

CHECK-UP

1 From where is the person making the phone call?
2 What is the person's name?
3 How many sheep have got loose?
4 Why are the Gardaí not having a good day?
5 Did anybody get hurt?

46 WEEK 12 • DAY 2

FOR SALE

For Sale

Playtendo Games Console with 10 Games

Only six months old, good as new

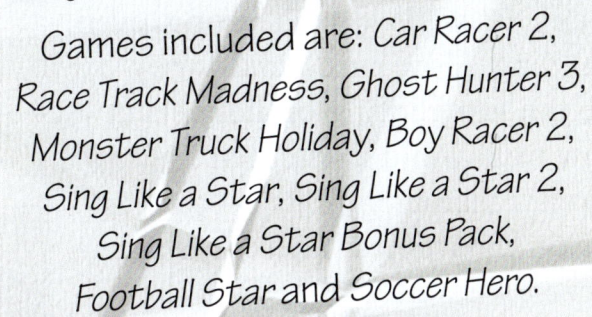

Games included are: Car Racer 2, Race Track Madness, Ghost Hunter 3, Monster Truck Holiday, Boy Racer 2, Sing Like a Star, Sing Like a Star 2, Sing Like a Star Bonus Pack, Football Star and Soccer Hero.

All games working fine and still in their cases.

Console includes two game pads, steering wheel kit and a microphone.

Only €199 for the lot.

Would also be willing to swap everything for a mountain bike or a two-person tent.

Phone Jack on 088 77432268910.

CHECK-UP

1. What is for sale?
2. How many games are included?
3. What extras come with the console?
4. Why is there a microphone included?
5. How much does the seller want for the set?
6. What would he be willing to swap everything for?
7. Name the person selling the games console.
8. How do you know that Jack is interested in racing cars?
9. What other sport do you think he might like?
10. Which game would be your favourite?

At the Gates

It was good to stand on solid ground after so long a voyage. The ships had been crowded and cramped. Now we stood, the whole Greek army, in lines facing the walls of the city. Thousands of us rested our spears and heavy shields on the sand. The sun beat down on us.

I looked towards the city. Its walls looked strong, even from where we were standing. How hard would they be to climb? I could see the sun glinting on helmets at the top of the walls. How well would these men fight to defend their city? Too well, I feared.

Our flags hung limply on their poles. There was not even the lightest of breezes. We waited.

At last, I saw movement off to my right. Our line parted and the king walked out with his guards. He headed straight for the city's huge wooden gates.

'Will you give me back my queen?' I heard him call to the men on the wall above him. 'Give me Helen and we will leave peacefully!'

I could not hear their answer. However, I could tell by the scowl on our king's face that he was not pleased. He stormed back to our lines, barking a sharp order as he passed.

'Begin!'

And so, we went to war with the city of Troy.

CHECK-UP

1 Where was the teller of the story from?
2 What questions were going through his mind as he looked at the city?
3 What was the weather like?
4 What weapons did the soldiers have?
5 What did the king want?

Wrong Number!

Mark got an odd text message on his mobile. Here is what it read:

> Loot in pipe at 26 Muck Rd. Get it & meet me outside Mac's Pet Shop at 8.00pm. Be there or else ... l

The text message was odd because it did not come from anybody that Mark knew.

Mark was curious. He cycled down to Muck Road on his bike and soon found number 26. There was no house there. It was still a building site. There was a broken orange pipe sticking up out of the ground. Mark pulled it up and shook it. Out fell a small canvas bag. When he opened the bag, he saw that it was full of diamonds!

Of course, Mark went straight to the Garda station.

'Good work young man!' said the Garda.

That evening, at 8.00pm, the stranger who had sent Mark the text message by mistake stood outside Mac's Pet Shop. He was waiting for his robber friend to arrive with the bag of diamonds. What a surprise he got when three big Gardaí jumped out of the pet shop and grabbed him!

The moral of this story is: always check the phone number before you press the 'send' button!

CHECK-UP

1 What is the boy's name?
2 What did the text message say?
3 Why did the boy find the text message odd?
4 What was in the bag?
5 What is the moral of the story?

Daisies

Most people have made, or have tried to make, a daisy chain. With their thin green stems, white petals and yellow flower heads, daisies are very popular wild flowers. They are also called '*Bellis*'. This means 'beautiful' in Latin.

Like a lot of flowers, daisies close their petals at night. When morning comes, they open out again. Their yellow heads soon attract bees.

Bees suck **nectar** from the daisy. This is a sweet drink that bees need. While drinking the nectar, tiny bits of yellow pollen from the daisy stick to the bee. Then the bee flies away to another daisy. When it lands, some pollen from the first daisy falls off its body. The second daisy is then **pollinated**.

When a flower is pollinated, it can grow seeds. The clever little daisy has spread its pollen without moving. The bee is happy too as it gets the nectar. The pollinated daisy soon loses its petals. Seeds then grow in its yellow head.

The wind blows the seeds all over the field or garden. The seeds lie on the ground until the next spring. Then the sun starts to warm the soil and the rain waters it. The tiny seeds start to grow. First the shoots grow, then the leaves and finally the flower. And the life cycle starts all over again.

CHECK-UP

1. What is the Latin word for daisy?
2. What does it mean?
3. What do bees suck from daisies?
4. What sticks to the bee's body?
5. What happens to the petals of pollinated daisies?

Questions

Who likes to swing from
The branch of a tree?
I Do!

Who likes cheeseburgers
With baked beans for tea?
I Do!

Who likes to watch
What comes on TV?
I Do!

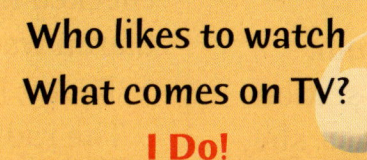

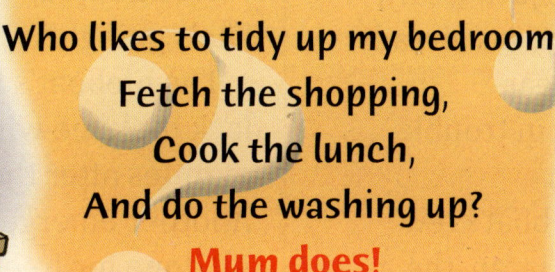

Who likes to tidy up my bedroom,
Fetch the shopping,
Cook the lunch,
And do the washing up?
Mum does!

Doesn't she?

By Trevor Harvey

Choose the correct answer.
1. The poet likes to swing from
   (a) the light or (b) a branch?
2. For tea, the poet likes
   (a) baked beans or (b) ice cream?
3. Who likes to do the cooking:
   (a) the poet, (b) Mum or (c) Dad?

CHECK-UP
1. What is the name of the poem?
2. Who wrote the poem?
3. What foods are mentioned in the poem?
4. What jobs are mentioned in the poem?
5. What does the poet like to eat with cheeseburgers?

Gone in Eight Minutes

Alison smiled at the visitor across the hotel desk.

'Now sir. Here is your key and ...' All of a sudden there was a buzzing sound. 'Excuse me, please', she said.

She glanced at the screen of her pager. It read:

Lifeboat launch

... and she ran.

The hotel was near the harbour. Alison sprinted to the lifeboat station in just over two minutes. Even so, she wasn't the first to arrive. Jack Healy, the coxswain, or skipper, was already putting on his survival gear.

'There's a fishing boat in trouble, Alison,' he explained.

Alison heard more lifeboat crew racing into the station. Ciaran, the engineer, had already fired up the boat's engines. He was preparing the lifeboat as the others quickly dressed. Jack spoke, 'Alison, you're on radio. Gary navigates, Colm and Stephen are with us.'

They all ran to the lifeboat. Everyone got aboard and strapped themselves into their seats. Alison set the radio to Emergency Channel 16. Gary checked the navigation computer. Ciaran watched the engine dials.

'Ready, Jack!'

The radio crackled. A frightened voice shouted, 'We are taking in water! She's going! ...'

The lifeboat's twin engines roared as Jack took the wheel. Seven and a half minutes after the call, they were off. Another emergency. More lives to save. All done for free by volunteers.

The lifeboat always leaves in less than eight minutes.

CHECK-UP

1. Where does Alison normally work?
2. How did she know there was an emergency?
3. Who was the coxswain of the lifeboat?
4. Are the members of the lifeboat crew paid for what they do?
5. What radio channel is kept for emergencies?

GROW YOUR OWN MONSTER

To grow your own monster, you will need a packet of monster seeds. You can get these at any good magic garden shop. If your aunt or uncle is a witch or a wizard, they might give you some too. You can grow lots of different kinds of monster. Favourites are Blue Furry, Howling Devil, Green Spotty and Blood Thirsty. Blue Furry monsters are nice, easy ones to grow if this is your first time. Howling Devil and Blood Thirsty monsters can be a bit tricky to care for once they start to grow. Be sure to get nice, fresh seeds.

Instructions

When and where to sow: any good garden soil between April and July, when there is a full moon.

How to sow: plant the seeds 10cm deep and 50cm apart to avoid overcrowding.

Sprouting time: seeds should start to sprout after about two weeks. The first arms and legs will start to grow after about a week.

Care and feeding: young monsters should be fed twice a week. They like fresh dragon blood for the first few weeks. When their mouths are big enough, they can be given pieces of meat. (Warning: always wear heavy gloves when feeding monsters. Even small monsters will bite.)

When ready: monsters will be fully grown by September or October. You will know they are grown when they dig their legs out of the ground and start chasing you.

Good luck!

CHECK-UP

1. Where can you get monster seeds?
2. What are the easiest monsters to grow?
3. How far apart should the seeds be planted?
4. What should you wear when feeding meat to monsters? Why?
5. Why do you think this story is pure fiction?

CHINESE DRAGONS

Dragons appear a lot in Chinese stories and poems. You will find pictures, statues, toys and puppets of dragons all over China. Where did the idea of dragons come from? They are only make-believe, aren't they?

Many years ago, Chinese people began to find the bones of giant animals under the ground. The bones were so old that they had turned to stone. These bones came from strange animals that no one had ever seen before. They had long necks, huge heads, terrible teeth and sharp claws. Dragons!

People began to make up stories about these strange animals. They said they were magic! They said they could fly! They said they could talk!

Many years later, people found out that dinosaurs had once lived on Earth. In fact, the bones that had been found in China all those years ago were really the fossils of dinosaurs. China is still a great place to go looking for dinosaur fossils. Some of the biggest dinosaurs ever found where in China.

Perhaps the Chinese people of long ago were not quite right when they thought that the dinosaurs were dragons. But it was a very good guess!

CHECK-UP

1. What fairy tale animal is seen a lot in China?
2. What did Chinese people find under the ground years ago?
3. What made people think these bones came from dragons?
4. What sort of stories did people make up?
5. What animals were the bones really from?

The Chuck Wagon Restaurant

Menu

Starters
Chicken wings
Soup of the day
Corn on the cob
Bean salad
Garlic bread
Baby fish cakes
Cheese ravioli
Tomato salad

Main Courses
Tender steak, cooked just how you like it
Pork chops in a spicy sauce
Chicken fillet stuffed with cheese
Homemade beef burgers in a toasted bun with cheese and bacon
Chuck's famous fish pie (choice fish pieces in a creamy sauce topped with potato)
Salmon steaks grilled with a little butter and pepper
Spicy meatballs and spaghetti
Cheese and onion pie

All the above are served with vegetables and a choice of French fries or mashed potatoes

Pizza with a choice of toppings: corn, ham, pepperoni, mushroom, onion, extra cheese, pineapple, tomatoes, peppers, tuna, spicy meatballs

Desserts
Ice cream: vanilla, strawberry, lemon, chocolate or blackberry

Double chocolate fudge pie with extra chocolate sauce

Apple pie with cream

Rhubarb crumble with custard

Fresh fruit salad

Drinks
Tea or coffee

Cola, orange, lemon and lime, water

CHECK-UP

1. How many starters are on the menu?
2. Name all the toppings you can choose for a pizza.
3. Which dishes would be good for someone who does not eat meat?
4. Which dish comes with a creamy sauce?
5. Which meal would you choose for yourself?

Monsters

There are lots of stories about monsters around the world. Some monsters are very famous. Let's take a look at a few of them.

The Loch Ness monster is supposed to live in the deep water of Loch Ness in Scotland. Lots of people say they have seen it. It is supposed to have a very long neck. This is meant to rise out of the water like a dinosaur as it swims along.

The people of Nepal in the Himalayan Mountains often talk about a shy, furry snow monster. They call it the **yeti**. Sometimes, people can get lost in snow storms on the mountain. Some say that the yeti has saved them from the cold. It sounds like a very helpful monster.

The yeti might have an American cousin called Big Foot. This is another shy, furry monster that likes to be left alone, people say. The only signs that the Big Foot leaves behind are footprints. Big ones!

It seems that there are no furry monsters in Ireland. Some people talk about banshees, however. These are supposed to be lady ghosts who haunt some families. It is said to be bad news if you hear a banshee screaming. Some people say they have heard a banshee. It is more likely that it was some man hitting his thumb with a hammer or a gust of wind. Who knows?

CHECK-UP

1 Where is the Loch Ness monster supposed to live?
2 Where is the yeti supposed to come from?
3 What is so helpful about the yeti?
4 Name another famous furry monster from America.
5 What do you not want to hear a banshee doing?

The Little Thief

When Mum lost her earrings, everyone had to help in the search. Things are always getting lost in our house. We all looked high and low. Even Jack helped. He's only two and a half and always wears his pirate hat. After an hour of pulling out drawers, emptying boxes and searching the couches, we gave up.

'They'll turn up,' said Dad. 'Now, has anyone seen my wedding ring? I left it on the bedside table.'

Of course nobody had, so the search began all over again. Everyone was fed up, except Pirate Jack. He was enjoying himself, running from room to room, pulling down all sorts of stuff, looking for the 'wing', as he called it.

After another hour of fruitless searching, Dad said he had to go to the bank. But he could not find his car keys. That's when I began to get suspicious. Jack was nowhere to be seen. He had toddled into his bedroom. I tiptoed after him and watched quietly. The little 'thief' lifted the corner of the carpet and dropped a bracelet through a small hole in the floorboards.

When he saw me, he pointed to the hole. 'Pirate Jack's treasure,' he grinned.

CHECK-UP

1 What did Mum lose first?
2 How old is Jack?
3 What does Jack always wear?
4 How long did they search for the ring before they gave up?
5 Where was Jack hiding the stolen goods?

Down By The Sea

Every day the tide goes in and out twice. The sea level rises on the beach at high tide, when the tide comes in. It falls low on the beach at low tide, when the tide goes out. Many creatures, particularly shellfish, live on or near the beach. There are many different kinds of shellfish.

When the tide goes out, some types of crab come out of the sea. They bury themselves in the sand or hide under a stone or a rock. If you turn over a stone on the beach, you might just see one. Crabs have ten legs and a hard outer shell. Their two front legs are **pincers**. Crabs use their pincers to catch food and tear it up before eating it. The other eight legs are used for moving. Crabs move sideways.

Another type of shellfish that lives on the seashore is the hermit crab. A hermit crab has a soft body. To protect itself, it lives in an empty shell. When it grows bigger, it must find a bigger shell to live in.

Cockles, mussels, oysters and scallops have hard shells. They cling onto rocks when the tide goes out so they are not washed out to sea. These shellfish are all called **molluscs**. They have two shells joined together. These shells can open and shut to allow them to feed as they are swimming along.

Most of the shells that you find on the seashore are, or once were, home to little sea creatures such as limpets, periwinkles or whelks. They are very like the snails which live in a shell on land.

CHECK-UP

1. How often does the tide go in and out every day?
2. How many legs do crabs have?
3. What do crabs use their pincers for?
4. What is a mollusc?
5. Name one land animal that lives in a shell.

How To Make A Paper Aeroplane

To make a paper aeroplane, you will need a piece of rectangular paper.

Instructions

1. Fold the paper in half down the middle (see picture 1). Make a strong crease. Then open the paper out again.
2. Fold the top left-hand corner as far as the middle crease (see picture 2). Make a strong crease.
3. Now fold the top right-hand corner in the same way (see picture 3).
4. Fold your page shut along the middle crease with the folded corners on the inside. Crease the middle fold strongly.
5. The top edges should line up with the bottom edges. Now fold the wings down, one at a time.
6. Unfold the wings to finish your paper aeroplane.

Operating Instructions

Hold the aeroplane by the middle crease with your thumb and first finger. Point the 'arrow' in the direction you want it to fly and launch it into the air.

CHECK-UP

1. Did your aeroplane fly?
2. What shape paper did you use to make it?
3. Why is it important to make strong creases in the paper?
4. When you launch it, what keeps the aeroplane in the air?
5. Does your aeroplane glide better than a bunched up piece of paper? Why?

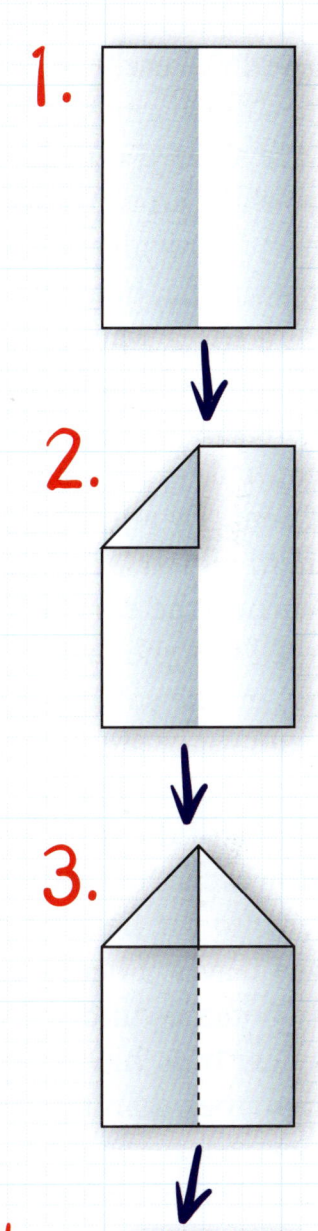

September 1847

Pat loved the early autumn mornings, the golden light and the soft mistiness bringing a glow to every single thing. He slipped quietly out of the cabin. His wife Kate and the children were still asleep. He loved the idea of his family being all snug and warm and safe together. Life was simple, but it was good.

It was a short walk to his field. He tended the small plot of land with Kate and the children every day. Sometimes he did a bit of work on the roads for the local council or for a big farmer to earn extra money for the rent. By and large, they did all right and the land kept them all fed. They had been lucky up to now.

Pat turned the corner in the lane leading to his field. The smell was the first thing that he noticed. It sat heavy and foul on the soft morning air, a sick rotten stench that could make a grown man gag. It was the **blight**!

His heart pounding in his chest, Pat ran into his field. Some of the lush, green potato plants still looked fine. However, the smell of rot almost made him sick. Further into the field, he could see wilted stalks and yellowed leaves. There was no hope of finding any healthy potatoes under them. He turned to the green plants near him, his mind racing. They always planted more potatoes than they needed for a year. There was still hope that he could save some of the crop.

He plunged his hands deep into the soft, brown earth that he and Kate had tended these past ten years. He hoped for the feel of firm, healthy potatoes still untouched by the blight.

His fingers found a soft, slimy mass. He pulled out one rotten potato, then another and another. He searched the whole drill, then the next and the next. The crop was gone.

His family would starve.

CHECK-UP

1. What time of year was it?
2. How did Pat feel leaving his home that morning?
3. What was his wife's name?
4. Did they own the field?
5. What had caused the potato crop to fail?

The Snake

Niall had his birthday party at Dublin Zoo. The best bit was when we got to visit the reptile house with Sally, the zookeeper. The house was really warm inside. We looked at the snakes and lizards in the glass cases. Then Sally smiled and opened one of the cases. We took a step back, feeling a little bit scared.

'Who would like to hold a snake?' she asked us.

We just looked at her like she was mad. Hold a snake? No one said anything. Then Niall spoke up.

'Eh. Won't it bite?'

'Not this fellow,' the zookeeper grinned. 'He is a young python. Only a baby, really.'

'Some baby!' said Laura. 'He's huge!'

'A fully grown python can be up to seven metres long,' Sally told us. 'Who wants to be first?'

'I'll try,' said Laura.

Sally put the snake across Laura's shoulders.

'This is great!' said Laura.

We all wanted to try then. I was next.

The python felt heavy. Its skin was smooth and dry. It looked at me with its dark eyes.

Its long tongue flicked and tickled my hand.

Maybe I'll be a zookeeper someday.

CHECK-UP

1. Whose birthday was it?
2. Where was the party held?
3. What was the zookeeper's name?
4. What kind of snake did they get to hold?
5. Who was the first one to hold the snake?

Blackbeard

Blackbeard was one of the most feared pirates of all time. His real name was Edward Teach. However, people knew him as Blackbeard. He made himself look really fierce in order to scare his victims. He had a wild black beard. Clouds of black smoke even seemed to swirl around his head. The black smoke came from smoking cannon fuses which he used to stuff into his pirate's hat. He was also armed to the teeth! He had daggers, pistols and cutlasses (curved swords that pirates loved).

Blackbeard showed no mercy. If you did not hand over your valuable rings quickly he would cut off your fingers. Every now and then he would make one of his crew walk the plank, just to remind them who was boss!

Blackbeard's ship was called the *Queen Anne's Revenge*. It had 40 cannon. It spread terror throughout the Caribbean Sea. However, in 1718, Blackbeard met his match. After a long fight, Lieutenant Robert Maynard of the Royal Navy managed to slay the fearsome pirate. Maynard cut off Blackbeard's head. He hung it from the prow of his own ship as a grim warning to other pirates of the high seas! Obviously, Maynard wasn't a very pleasant person either!

CHECK-UP

1. What was Blackbeard's real name?
2. What weapons did he carry?
3. Why did he sometimes make one of his crew walk the plank?
4. What was the name of his ship?
5. Who finally killed him and in what year did this happen?

School Timetable

Monday is the pits,
it's always wet and grey.
Tuesday is no better,
another working day.
On Wednesday I start to hope
that the week is halfway through.
But my hopes are dashed on Thursday
when there's still so much to do.
Friday is a blur
of tests, art and P.E.
Then that school bell gives a ring
and for two whole days I'm FREE!

By Jim Halligan

CHECK-UP
1. Does the child in the poem like Monday? Why?
2. Is Tuesday any better?
3. What makes Wednesday seem a little bit better?
4. Why is Thursday not great?
5. What happens on Friday?
6. What marks the beginning of two days of freedom?

SETANTA

There is an old Irish legend about a boy called Setanta. His uncle was Conor MacNassa, the King of Ulster. Conor led a group of soldiers called the Red Branch Knights. It was every boy's dream to become one of these fine soldiers. When he was quite young, Setanta went to live in Conor's fort to train to be a Red Branch Knight.

One night, Conor was going to a feast in the house of his friend, Culann. He invited Setanta to join him. The boy said he would follow on later because he wanted to finish a hurling match. Setanta loved hurling and did not want to miss the game.

Conor went to the feast. He soon forgot that Setanta was following him later. This was a big mistake. Culann let loose his fierce guard dog to watch over his home, as he did every night.

The feast was in full swing when everybody heard a terrible noise outside. Conor remembered Setanta at last! Everyone rushed outside. They were afraid that they would see the boy killed by the huge dog.

Luckily, Setanta was fine. He had been attacked by the dog and had to kill it with his hurley and ball. Poor Culann was very upset. He had lost his fine guard dog. Setanta was very sorry about the dog. He said he would guard Culann's house just as the dog had done. From then on, he was called Cú Chulainn (*Koo Kullin*), which means 'Hound of Culann'. He became a great hero when he grew up. ■

CHECK-UP

1. What was the name of Setanta's uncle?
2. What group of soldiers did he lead?
3. What did Culann use to guard his home at night?
4. What happened outside the house?
5. What did Setanta do to make it up to Culann?

Green Fingers

Michael hadn't seen his Uncle Roger since he was a toddler. He couldn't remember him at all. Mum and Michael were in the car on their way to visit him.

'You will have great fun playing with your cousin, Tessa, in Uncle Roger's garden,' Mum told him. 'Roger has green fingers.'

'He has?' said Michael. He was suddenly very interested.

Uncle Roger was weeding the garden when they arrived. He was wearing gardening gloves. Michael felt too shy to ask him to take them off.

The garden was great. There were flowers everywhere and great climbing trees. There was even a path down to a stream with stepping stones. Cousin Tessa was great fun. She was a real tomboy.

'Does your Dad have green fingers?' Michael asked her.

'Everyone says that about him,' said Tessa, and she ran off.

When they came in from the garden all dirty, Mum and Uncle Roger were chatting. He had his hands in his pockets so Michael still couldn't see his fingers. It wasn't until they drove off that Uncle Roger took his hands out of his pockets to wave goodbye. What a disappointment!

'It's a lie!' said Michael crossly. 'His fingers aren't green.'

Mum was silent for a moment. Then she burst out laughing. Michael didn't understand what she found so funny. He wasn't one bit pleased. ■

CHECK-UP

1 Why could Michael not remember Uncle Roger?
2 What was special about Uncle Roger, according to Mum?
3 Describe Uncle Roger's garden.
4 Why could Michael not see Uncle Roger's fingers when he arrived?
5 What does it mean to have green fingers?

Frogs

Frogs have a very interesting life cycle. In the springtime, female frogs lay lots of eggs in shallow ponds. These eggs look like little black dots in a soft, gooey jelly. This is called **frogspawn**. The frogspawn protects the tiny eggs.

After about ten days, tadpoles hatch out of the eggs. It is hard to imagine that these tiny dots with tails will grow into frogs.

Tadpoles live off the plants and tiny insects that live in the pond. After about 40 days, the tadpoles begin to grow back legs. Their tails get shorter and skin grows over their gills.

After another two weeks, their front legs start to grow. They now breathe through their lungs. This means that they cannot stay under water all of the time. They must come up to the surface for air.

It takes another three weeks before the tadpole has changed completely into a baby frog (froglet). It now has no tail. It lives in and out of the water. It can also hop about. It eats insects, slugs and worms.

When the cold days of winter come, frogs hibernate in the mud at the bottom of the pond. The next spring, female frogs will lay lots of eggs and the cycle starts all over again!

CHECK-UP

1. At what time of the year does the female frog lay eggs?
2. Describe frogspawn.
3. What do tadpoles eat?
4. What is a baby frog called?
5. What do frogs eat?

OOPS!

Do you ever look at road signs? Some are quite funny. Here are a few examples.

The first road sign is from a town in County Clare. It says it all! The second sign shows just how important it is to learn your spellings. The third sign is on a very musical road! The fourth sign is definitely not a sign from Ireland.

Here are some more rather silly signs from around the world. If you look for them, you will probably spot a few yourself. Some signs are only silly if you are in a bit of a silly mood yourself!

CHECK-UP

1 What should the signs with the spelling mistakes really say?
2 How many signs can you see in picture number 1?
3 What is strange about the 'Keep Right' sign?
4 What animals should you beware of?
5 To where are the elderly people being directed?

AESOP

Aesop was a Greek writer. He was famous for his 'fables'. Here are two of his fables. Both have a message/moral.

THE FOX AND THE CROW

One day, a crow stole a tasty piece of meat. The crow flew to the top of a tree to enjoy the meat in peace. Then along came a fox. The fox saw the meat in the crow's beak. He thought he would like it for himself.

'Oh crow,' he called out to the crow. 'What a beautiful bird you are. Such fine wings, such shiny feathers! Is your voice as beautiful as the rest of you?'

The crow was very flattered. To show the fox what a beautiful voice she had, she let out a loud CAW. The meat dropped out of the crow's open beak into the waiting jaws of the fox at the bottom of the tree.
The moral of the fable is: Beware of flattery! ('Flattery' is false praise.)

CHECK-UP

1. Where did the crow go to eat the meat?
2. What happened when the crow opened her beak?
3. Was the fox telling the truth?

THE FOX AND THE GRAPES

A very hungry fox saw some mouth-watering grapes high up on the vine. He just had to have some! So he jumped as high as he could. However, he could not reach even the lowest grape. He stood on his hind legs but still could not reach high enough. He jumped again and again but he did not succeed. No matter how hard he tried, he just could not reach those juicy grapes.

At last he gave up. Turning away, he hid his disappointment by saying 'those grapes were sour anyway, not worth having!'
The moral of the fable is: A fool rubbishes the things he cannot have.

CHECK-UP

1. What fruit did the fox see?
2. Why could he not get them?
3. What is the moral of this fable? Explain your answer.

Survivor

Sarah felt the press and weight of her body on the wet, hard sand beneath her. Cold water lapped and swirled around her feet. She opened her eyes and slowly, painfully raised her head. It took a little time for the world to come into focus. She could taste salt on her lips. With a low groan, she rolled over and sat up.

She was on a beach with silvery sand. Sparkling blue water lapped in gentle waves against it. Bright sunshine poured down from a clear blue sky. It warmed her. Further up the beach, the sand gave way first to scrubby plants and then to trees. Sarah stared around her, dazed. She tried to take it all in. She wiped dry sand from her cheek.

And then she remembered …

… struggling to get into her life jacket … howling wind beating rain into her face … Dad firing the emergency flare into the dark sky … Mum pushing the life-raft into the raging sea.

Her name was Sarah Dunne. She was eight years old. She lived in Galway with her parents Mark and Sue. They were on a sailing holiday off the north coast of Australia. Four days into the trip, a storm had caught them. They had no time to find a safe harbour.

She had no idea how she had ended up on this beach. She did not know where she was or where her parents were. What would she do? ■

CHECK-UP

1 What was the girl's name?
2 How did she feel?
3 Where was she from?
4 What had the family been doing?
5 What had happened while they were at sea?

A Plant That Can Count?

Some people think that ducks can count. It helps them to mind their ducklings. But what about a plant that can count?

The Venus Fly Trap is a plant. It grows in wet marshy places. There is very little goodness in marshy soil so many plants find it hard to grow there. Any plant that can find an extra supply of food for itself will grow better. The Venus Fly Trap gets extra food by catching insects.

Each leaf of the plant is like two hands that can snap together when an insect lands on it. Once the insect is trapped, the leaf is able to slowly digest it. The goodness it gets from the dead insect will help it to grow.

The plant seems to have a clever trick to make sure its leaves don't just snap shut every time the wind blows. It can count to three! Every leaf has tiny hairs that can feel when an insect lands on it. The insect touches a hair once but nothing happens. It touches a hair a second time but nothing happens. Then, it touches a hair the third time. SNAP! The leaves snap shut and the plant gets lunch!

CHECK-UP

1 In what type of place does the Venus Fly Trap live?
2 Why does the plant need to catch insects?
3 What part of the plant catches insects?
4 How much can it count up to?
5 What are on the leaves to help the plant to count?

Dog

Dog day
Dog lead
Dog beg
Dog whine
Dog walk
Dog bark
Dog go running in the park

Dog snooze
Dog nap
Dog snort
Dog scratch
Dog sneeze
Dog howl
Dog see postman, start to growl

Dog sniff
Dog tooth
Dog chew
Dog bone
Dog stretch
Dog roll
Dog gulp food right out of bowl

Dog paddle
Dog shake
Dog leg
Dog tail
Dog ear
Dog end
Dog will always be my friend

By Jim Halligan

CHECK-UP

1. What does the dog do to get a walk in the park?
2. Does the dog like the postman? Explain your answer.
3. Does the dog eat its food slowly? Explain your answer.
4. Name all the sounds the dog makes.
5. What parts of a dog are mentioned in the poem?

The Lost City of Atlantis

More than 2,000 years ago, people in Greece were telling stories about a city called Atlantis. It was a beautiful place with fine buildings and lovely gardens. The people of Atlantis were said to be the best builders who had ever lived. Then, in the space of one day and one night, the whole city is said to have sunk beneath the sea. Everyone who lived there perished.

Over the years, many people have looked for the lost city of Atlantis. However, no one has ever found it. Some think that it was all just a story. Other people are not so sure. There are lots of ideas about what might have happened to the city.

Some say that a huge volcano erupted. This caused a giant tidal wave that swept the city into the sea. Others say that a terrible earthquake made the land sink, bringing the city with it. Nobody is certain about what actually happened.

The strange thing is that divers have found old stone buildings at the bottom of the sea near Greece. They have also found some more buildings off the coast of America. Nobody can say how the buildings got there. One thing is sure, however. These buildings must have been on land at some time, long ago.

Maybe there was a city called Atlantis after all.

CHECK-UP

1. How old are the stories about the city of Atlantis?
2. What do the stories say about what happened to the city?
3. Has anyone ever found the city?
4. What might have happened to the city?
5. What has been found that shows that Atlantis might have existed?

The Puppy Campaign

Snoop had two puppies during the night.

'It could have been worse,' said Dad. 'She could have had ten!'

Paul wished that there had been ten puppies. They were so cute and plump and cuddly.

Jenny was already working out how they could persuade Dad and Mum to keep them.

'Eight weeks at most,' explained Dad. 'Then they go to new homes.'

'We will see about that,' whispered Jenny to her brother.

Every day, the puppies got cuter. They tumbled around the kitchen, yapping and getting under everyone's feet.

'Please, please can we keep them,' the children begged.

Mum was the first to crack.

'One would be nice,' she said. She picked up fluffy little George, who licked her nose. Jenny looked at Paul. Round one to the children. One day, Sarah from next door asked if she could have Mandy, the puppy with the black ears. This was nearly as good as keeping her themselves. Dad was not happy though. 'Who will clean up after George? And take him for walks?' he asked.

'We will,' said Paul and Jenny together.ABad did not look convinced. Then Mum blurted out, 'We promise!'

Dad's mouth fell open. Then he smiled.

'Game, set and match,' whispered Jenny, winking at her brother.

CHECK-UP

1 What was the name of the mother dog?
2 How many puppies did she have?
3 Which parent was the first to crack?
4 What did Mum say that surprised Dad so much?
5 From what sport does the phrase 'Game, set and match' come?

Ants

Ants are tiny insects. They are very busy and well-organised insects. They live in **colonies**. There can be many thousands of ants living in a colony. Their nests can be made of twigs and leaves. Some nests are built underground and they can be very big. The ants leave twigs and soil at the entrance. This forms an ant hill. If you could see inside a nest, you would see a maze of passages and little rooms.

In the ant colony, each ant has a job to do.

- **The queen ant**: her job is to lay eggs. She spends her whole life laying many thousands of eggs. She is usually the mother of all the ants in the colony.
- **The male ants**: for a short time each year, the male ants fly in a swarm (big cloud of ants) and find a female ant. After this flight they will die.
- **The worker ants**: the worker ants do all the chores in the colony. They also look after the young ants. All the worker ants are female. Unlike the males and the queen, they have no wings.

Ants help each other out. If the food they want to carry back to the colony is too big or heavy, they break it up into smaller pieces. They then form a line to carry it home. Ants mostly eat leaves and fungi.

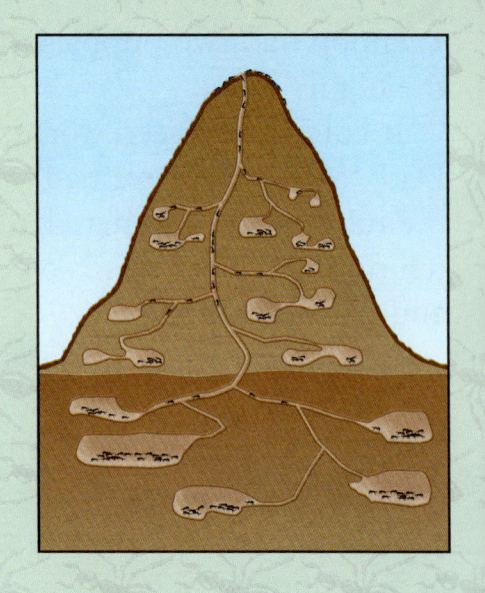

CHECK-UP

1. What is a group of ants called?
2. What would you see in an ant's nest if you could see inside?
3. What is the queen ant's job?
4. Are the worker ants male or female?
5. Why can't worker ants fly?

Chocolate Rice Krispies Cakes

To make chocolate Rice Krispies cakes, you will need:

- A big bowl
- A big saucepan
- Paper bun cases (at least 15)
- A wooden spoon
- A teaspoon
- A weighing scales
- An adult to help

Ingredients
100g Rice Krispies (or Cornflakes if you prefer them)
250g chocolate

Instructions

1. Break the chocolate into the bowl.
2. Melt the chocolate in the bowl over a saucepan of simmering water. Stir the chocolate with the wooden spoon to help it to melt.
   Note: You will need an adult to help you when melting the chocolate.
3. Take the bowl of melted chocolate away from the saucepan. Add the Rice Krispies (or Cornflakes). Stir the mixture until they are covered in chocolate.
4. Spoon the mixture into the paper cases.
5. Leave them in a cool place until they are set.
6. Clean up the mess and enjoy your Rice Krispies cakes!

CHECK-UP

1. Why do you need a weighing scales?
2. How much chocolate should you use?
3. How much Rice Krispies should you use?
4. How do you melt the chocolate?
5. Why do you think we use a wooden spoon for stirring hot mixtures?
6. Why must you have an adult to help you when melting the chocolate?
7. Why should you be the one who cleans up the mess?
8. Did you enjoy your Rice Krispies cakes?

Bones

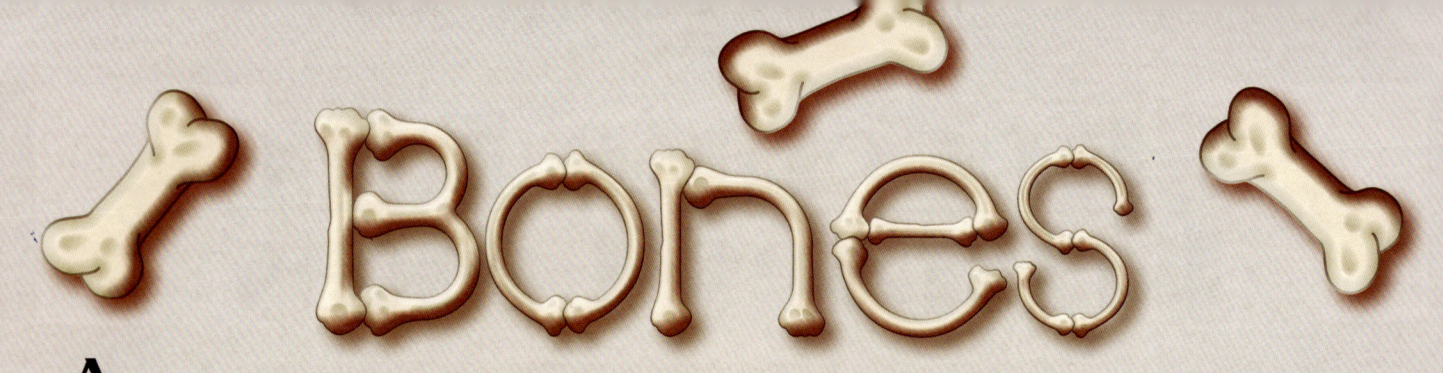

All humans and most animals have lots of bones and joints in their bodies. Without bones and joints, we could not stand, run, walk or even sit down.

1. **The skeleton**: an adult human skeleton has about 206 bones. A baby has about 270 bones. Some of the baby's bones join together as they get older.
2. **The bones**: our bones keep us upright. They also protect all the vital organs inside our bodies.
3. **The joints**: the place where one bone meets another is called a joint. There are a few different types of joints.
   - Ball and socket joint: this allows the bones at the joint to turn all around. Humans have them in their shoulders and hips.
   - Hinge joint: this allows the bones at the joint to bend forward and back like a door. Humans have them in their elbows and knees.
   - Cup joint: this is quite like the ball and socket joint. Humans have them in their wrists and ankles.
   - The swivel joint: this allows humans to turn their necks.
4. **The longest bone**: the femur (or thigh bone) is the longest bone in the body.
5. **The smallest bone**: the stirrup bone is the smallest bone in the body. It is found in the ear.

Match these bones
Can you match the common name of these bones to their real name? (Hint: the picture should help you.)

- Thigh bone • • Cranium
- The skull • • Vertebral column
- The backbone • • Tibia
- The shin bone • • Sternum
- The breast bone • • Femur

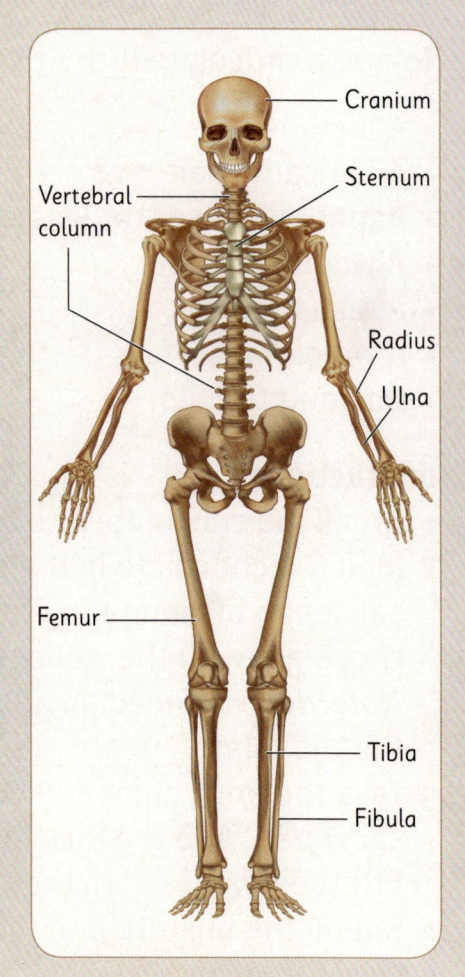

CHECK-UP
1. How many bones does an adult have?
2. How many bones does a baby have?
3. Where do you find joints in the body?
4. What type of joint is found in these parts of the body: elbow, neck, ankle and shoulder?
5. Name the longest and the smallest bones in the body.

Cat Trouble

Salem is a big softy of a cat. He is black and white. He loves to eat and sleep. He has a great life except for one thing. He does not like the cat next door. Salem and Tabby Tom just don't get on.

Last week, they had a really big fight. Salem came off worse. He slinked in the back door and kept licking his front paw. The next day, we could all see why. His paw was very swollen. He could not walk on it. Mam decided he needed to go to the vet, so Dad brought him.

I helped to get Salem into the cat box. He hates it so it was not easy. Then we put him into the car. He hissed and scratched all the way to the vet's surgery. He went very quiet when we got there, however. He knew where he was and he really wasn't pleased.

Peter, the vet, looked at his paw.

'It is a bite,' he said, showing us the teeth marks. 'I will need to operate in order to clean the wound.'

Poor Salem had to be put under for a short while. The wound was then cleaned by the vet. Salem was feeling very sorry for himself when we brought him home. Maybe he will be a bit more careful when he comes up against Tabby Tom the next time. ■

CHECK-UP

1. What colour is the main cat in the story?
2. What is the other cat's name?
3. What was wrong with Salem's paw?
4. Where did Dad have to take him?
5. How did Salem show that he was not happy in the car?

CAT AND MOUSE

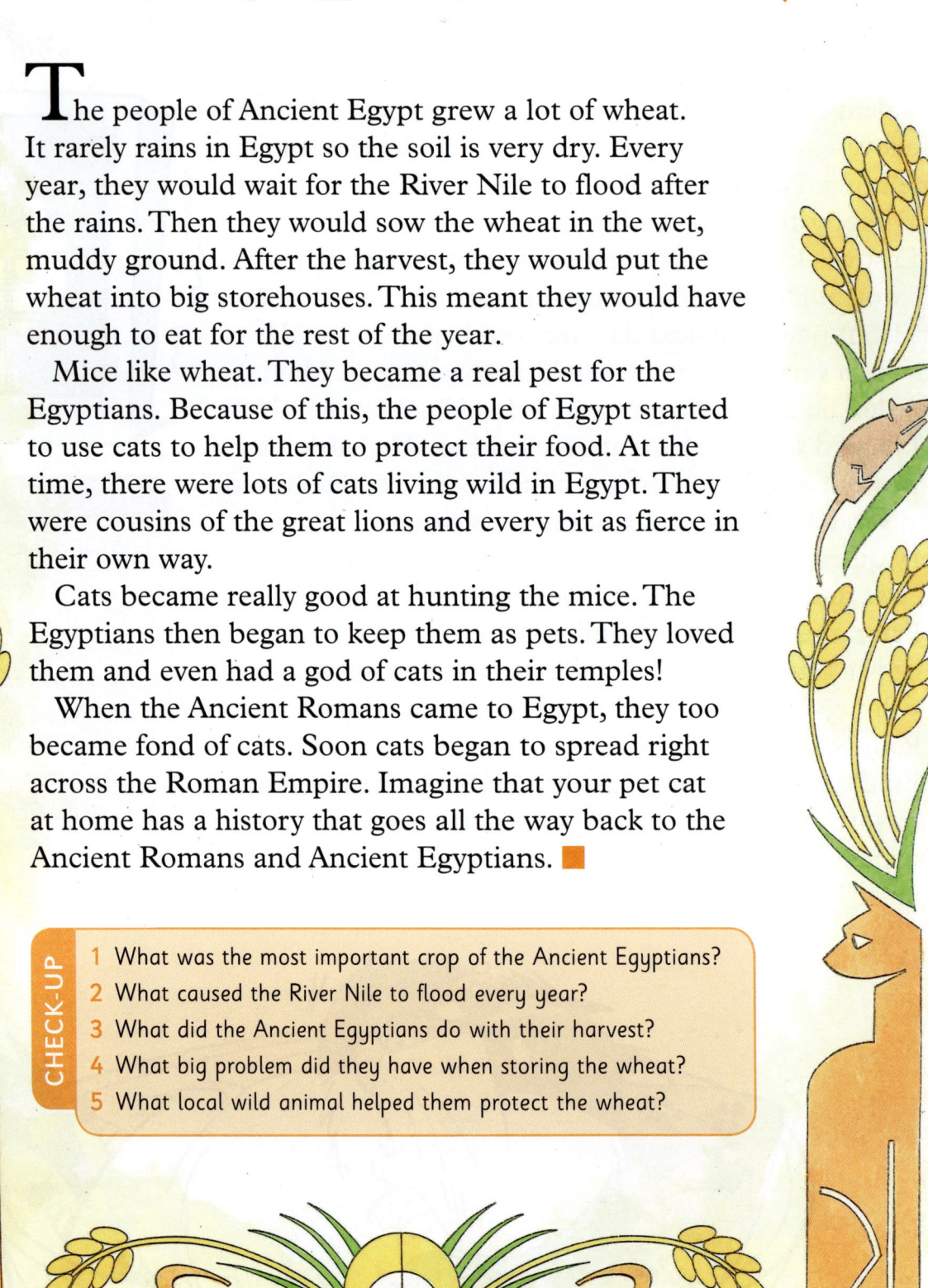

The people of Ancient Egypt grew a lot of wheat. It rarely rains in Egypt so the soil is very dry. Every year, they would wait for the River Nile to flood after the rains. Then they would sow the wheat in the wet, muddy ground. After the harvest, they would put the wheat into big storehouses. This meant they would have enough to eat for the rest of the year.

Mice like wheat. They became a real pest for the Egyptians. Because of this, the people of Egypt started to use cats to help them to protect their food. At the time, there were lots of cats living wild in Egypt. They were cousins of the great lions and every bit as fierce in their own way.

Cats became really good at hunting the mice. The Egyptians then began to keep them as pets. They loved them and even had a god of cats in their temples!

When the Ancient Romans came to Egypt, they too became fond of cats. Soon cats began to spread right across the Roman Empire. Imagine that your pet cat at home has a history that goes all the way back to the Ancient Romans and Ancient Egyptians.

CHECK-UP
1. What was the most important crop of the Ancient Egyptians?
2. What caused the River Nile to flood every year?
3. What did the Ancient Egyptians do with their harvest?
4. What big problem did they have when storing the wheat?
5. What local wild animal helped them protect the wheat?

WORLD TOP TENS

	Largest Countries	Largest Islands	Largest Lakes*	Countries with the Most People
1	Russia	Greenland	Caspian Sea	China
2	Canada	New Guinea	Lake Superior	India
3	USA	Borneo	Lake Victoria	USA
4	China	Madagascar	Lake Huron	Indonesia
5	Brazil	Baffin Island	Lake Michigan	Brazil
6	Australia	Sumatra	Lake Tanganyika	Pakistan
7	India	Honshu	Lake Baikal	Nigeria
8	Argentina	Victoria Island	Great Bear Lake	Russia
9	Kazakhstan	Great Britain	Lake Malawi	Bangladesh
10	Sudan / Algeria	Ellesmere Island	Great Slave Lake	Japan

Note: The Aral Sea was the fourth largest lake in the world. It has been shrinking since the 1960s. This is because the rivers that fed it were diverted. By 2007, it had declined to 10% of its original size. There is a lot of work being done to save the Aral Sea.

CHECK-UP

1 What lake and island share a girl's name?
2 What is the world's largest country?
3 What lake has an animal in its name?
4 Name the countries that appear in more than one list.
5 What lake has been shrinking since the 1960s?

Carrauntoohill

Carrauntoohill, in County Kerry, is the highest mountain in Ireland. It is 1,038 metres high. That is more than a kilometre! It is part of the Macgillycuddy's Reeks mountain range. The nearest large town is Killarney. There is a big metal cross on the **summit** (top) of the mountain. The cross is five metres high.

Many people visit Kerry to see the lovely mountains, lakes and valleys there. Some people like to climb the mountains. Carrauntoohill is a favourite one to try. It is not an easy mountain to climb, however, and only the best climbers should try it.

There are lots of steep, tricky parts to get past on the mountain. Some of these even have scary names like the Devil's Ladder or the Hag's Glen. The weather can be a problem too. Thick clouds can roll in from the Atlantic Ocean and these are like the thickest fog. Climbers often cannot see where they are going. Sometimes people get hurt on the mountain because of this.

If there is an accident, some very brave people will go to help hurt climbers. This group is called The Kerry Mountain Rescue Team. These heroes know the mountain better than anybody. They will find and help anyone who is lost or hurt on the mountain.

CHECK-UP

1. Name the highest mountain in Ireland.
2. Where is it found and how high is it?
3. What is found at the summit of the mountain?
4. Name some of the scary parts of the mountain.
5. Who comes to help people who are in trouble on the mountain?

Snow

It snowed all night long. In the morning, the whole place was white. Roger jumped out of bed and raced down the stairs.

'I'm going out,' he shouted.

'Not in your pyjamas,' said Mum.

So Roger had to get dressed and then wait, jumping up and down, while his Mum wrapped him up in warm clothes. She put on a hat, scarf, gloves, a big, heavy coat, thick socks and wellies before he could go outside to the snow.

In the field behind his house, Roger started rolling a snowball. He rolled it and rolled it, across the field and up the hill. The snowball got bigger and bigger and bigger. It was bigger than Roger, but still he rolled it up the hill. At last he got to the top of the hill. The snowball was huge. Roger was exhausted.

All of a sudden, the giant snowball began to roll down the other side of the hill. Down and down it went. Faster and faster. Getting bigger and bigger.

'Watch out,' shouted Roger, but it was too late. The snowball rolled right over a sheep and swept it along. Then it rolled over a sheepdog and picked him up too. Next it gathered up a farmer, and then a cow. Roger had to cover his eyes as the enormous snowball rolled across the farmyard, picking up a pig and a few hens on its way. It disappeared through the open door of the barn, crashing into the hay.

Roger did not stay around to see what happened next. He raced down his side of the hill and back into his own house.

'Had enough of the snow already?' asked Mum.

'Yes,' said Roger. 'Plenty!'

CHECK-UP

1. For how long did it snow?
2. Why did Mum stop Roger from going straight out?
3. Why was he jumping up and down?
4. Why did the snowball get bigger as it rolled down the hill?
5. Do you think this could really happen? Explain.

Snakes

Many people are scared of snakes. However, most snakes are harmless. In fact, they are quite amazing animals. They can swim. They can climb. They can crawl. But they have no legs!

Snakes are **reptiles**. Their skin is covered in **scales**. Snakes shed this skin when it becomes worn. This is called **moulting**. Young snakes moult a few times a year. Older snakes might only moult once a year.

Snakes have forked tongues, which they use to smell with. They use this to sense their prey. They have no eyelids so their eyes are always open. Their pupils look like slits. They have no ears but can sense sounds in the ground. This helps them to hunt.

Snakes cannot chew. They always swallow their food whole. They have teeth but these are curved. Some snakes have sharp **fangs** at the front of their mouths. Fangs are sharp, long, hollow teeth. They are linked to sacs that produce a poison called **venom**.

Some snakes are very dangerous. For example, vipers squirt poisonous venom to kill their prey. Pythons wrap themselves around their prey, squeezing them to death. The huge green anaconda is one of the largest snakes in the world. It can be up to five metres long. It can catch and squeeze to death animals such as deer, jaguars and even crocodiles. Anacondas live in rivers in South America.

CHECK-UP

1 How many legs do snakes have?
2 What happens to their skin?
3 How does a viper kill its prey?
4 How does a python kill its prey?
5 Where does the green anaconda live?

Banana Bread

For this recipe, you will need:
- 225g self-raising flour
- 100g soft brown sugar   • 100g butter
- 150g raisins   • 3 bananas (mashed)
- 2 eggs   • 2 tablespoons honey

Important: Ask an adult to help you.

Method
1. Place the flour and butter into a large bowl.
2. Rub them together with your fingers until the mixture is nice and crumbly.
3. Add the raisins and sugar to the mixture. Stir it all with a wooden spoon.
4. Add the honey and eggs to the mixture. Stir it well.
5. Stir in the mashed bananas.
6. Grease a baking tin (loaf size) with some butter.
7. Pour the mixture into the tin.
8. Bake the banana bread for one hour in a hot oven (gas mark 4, 180°C).
9. Take it out of the oven when it is cooked.
10. Leave it to cool before eating it.

CHECK-UP
1. What is this recipe for?
2. How much sugar is needed?
3. How many bananas are needed?
4. What do you use to rub the flour and butter together?
5. What is the last thing to be added to the mixture?
6. Should the bananas be chopped or mashed?
7. How do you make sure that the bread does not stick to the baking tin?
8. How long do you bake the bread for?
9. How hot must the oven be?
10. Why must you let the bread cool before eating it?

WEEK 21 • DAY 3

Christopher Columbus

Many years ago, people used to think that the world was flat. They were afraid to sail too far out to sea in case they sailed right off the edge of the world.

One man who did not believe this was Christopher Columbus. He was an Italian explorer who worked for the Spanish Queen. He wanted to prove that the world was round. He said that he would sail out into the Atlantic Ocean as far as he could go. In those days, spices from Asia were very important. It was very dangerous sailing to Asia around the tip of Africa. Columbus thought that if he sailed westwards from Spain he would reach India more easily.

In 1492, Queen Isabella of Spain gave Columbus three small ships to go on his voyage. They were called the *Niña*, the *Pinta* and the *Santa Maria*. Sailors were afraid to sail on this voyage as they believed they would starve to death or fall off the edge of the earth.

The ships sailed for five long weeks, going further and further away from Spain. The sailors were getting more and more afraid. They decided to throw Columbus overboard and steal the ships. He told them he would turn back if they did not spot land within three days. On the second last day, the lookout on the *Pinta* shouted out, 'Land! Land!'

The sailors forgot about throwing Columbus overboard. He was their hero now. They had reached land safely. They thought they were in Asia. In fact, Columbus had discovered the continent of America.

CHECK-UP

1. What did people think would happen if they sailed too far out to sea?
2. Which Queen gave Columbus ships to explore the seas with?
3. Name these three ships.
4. Where did Columbus think they had landed?
5. What continent did they discover?

Fireworks

We waited in the dark with Mam, huddled in our coats against the cold. We were on the road that ran by the river. Mam said we would have a good view from there. Other people waited further along. I could hear the river water lapping against the wall beside us.

'There!' Mam pointed suddenly across the river.

Sssshhhhhhhkkk! A dot of light shot up into the sky, making a sound like tearing cloth. Then it burst into a thousand sparks. The waiting crowd cheered. We heard the bang after the explosion. First the flash and the bang would follow.

So many flashes followed. The fireworks shot up in streams of red, green, blue and dazzling white. The air popped, flashed and banged. Small clouds of gunpowder smoke hung in the air. Some rockets exploded into hundreds of shards of light. These then exploded into even more sparks with a loud crackle. I loved those but the best firework came at the very end of the show.

One last huge rocket shot up and bloomed into an enormous ball of light. We all stood there spellbound until Mam said 'Come on, guys. Time to go home.'

CHECK-UP

1. What was happening in this story?
2. At what time of day did it happen?
3. Who brought the children to see the show?
4. What colours are mentioned in this story?
5. Which came first, the flash or the bang?

Vikings

Long ago, the people who lived in Norway, Sweden and Denmark were called the Norse. They were good at sailing, fishing and trading. Life in these countries was hard. The weather was often very cold and the winters long. Also, it was hard to grow food on the land. Some Norse people decided to give up fishing and farming. They became invaders and robbers. They called themselves Vikings.

The Vikings began to raid other countries. They robbed and killed lots of people. They were very frightening.

In around 795 AD, they reached Ireland in their great longships. For years, they attacked Irish churches and monasteries looking for gold. The monks had a lot of valuable religious items. They built high round towers to hide them from the raiders. In those days, the ordinary Irish people did not use money so there was not much gold for the Vikings to steal.

After a while, some of the Vikings decided to stay in Ireland and settle down. The land was very good for growing food. Other Norse people came to join them. They set up some of the first towns in Ireland such as Dublin, Wexford and Waterford. They traded goods that they made, such as pots and jewellery.

Many people in Ireland have a little bit of Viking in their family tree! ■

CHECK-UP

1. Where did the Norse people live long ago?
2. What did some Norse people become?
3. When did they begin to raid Ireland?
4. Was it worthwhile robbing ordinary Irish people? Why?
5. Name some towns that the Vikings started in Ireland.

The Best Garlic Bread Ever

When Italian people make garlic bread, they use olive oil instead of butter. Here is how they make it.

You will need:
- Fresh white bread – baguettes are good for this recipe
- A cup of olive oil
- Some garlic cloves
- A pinch of sea salt
- An adult to help you!

Method:
1. Cut the bread into thick slices.
2. Chop the garlic into small pieces. You might need help with this or you could use garlic paste.
3. Squish the garlic in a bowl with a pinch of sea salt. Add this to the olive oil.
4. Stir the garlic into the olive oil. Leave it for about half an hour (or longer if you can). This lets the taste of the garlic mix with the oil.
5. Place the slices of bread on a grill tray.
6. Spread the olive oil and garlic mixture onto the slices of bread.
7. Let the oil soak into the bread.
8. Ask an adult to put the tray of bread under the hot grill for a couple of minutes until the oil begins to sizzle. Be careful and do not let the little pieces of garlic go brown.
9. Ask the adult to take the garlic bread from under the grill. Place the slices on a plate.
10. Enjoy it with your family.

CHECK-UP

1. What type of oil is used to make this garlic bread?
2. How do you prepare the garlic?
3. Why do you leave the garlic and oil for a while before putting it on the bread?
4. Why should an adult help you with this recipe?
5. How long does it take for the garlic bread to cook under the grill?

BRIAN BORU

Brian Boru was born more than a thousand years ago. He and his big brother, Mahon, grew up in County Clare. In those days, Ireland was not at all like it is today. It was broken up into many small kingdoms. A local king ruled over each kingdom.

At this time, the Vikings had taken over parts of Ireland. There were many battles being fought throughout the land. Vikings had killed Brian's mother and many of his family and friends when he was young. Brian disliked the Vikings and wanted to run them out of Ireland.

He was very good at fighting in battles. He even fought with his brother Mahon at times! He was a good leader and won lots of battles. Eventually, he was made the King of Munster. A few years later, after winning more battles, he was made the High King of Ireland.

Trouble was never very far away. The Vikings in Dublin and the rest of Ireland did not like Brian. They got more Vikings to come over to Ireland for a big battle to overthrow Brian. The Viking army landed at Clontarf in Dublin in 1014. Brian's army was waiting for them. There was a terrible battle. Brian's army fought hard and drove the Vikings away. As they were retreating, however, one of the Vikings saw Brian and killed him. Brian Boru is still remembered as a hero. ∎

CHECK-UP
1. In what county did Brian Boru grow up?
2. What happened to his mother when he was young?
3. Was Brian a good leader? How do you know?
4. Where did the Viking army land in 1014?
5. What happened to Brian just after the battle?

Spoilt Girl

Aoife was spoilt. If she did not get her way, she sulked. If that did not work, she screamed. One day, she screamed so loudly that she broke a glass vase!

When Mammy went to hospital to have a baby, Aunt Kate came to look after Aoife. That day, she made Aoife potatoes, carrots and fish for dinner.

'I don't eat potatoes,' said Aoife. 'I want chips.'

'Oh dear,' said Aunt Kate and took the potatoes away.

'I don't eat carrots either,' whinged Aoife. 'Take them away!'

So Aunt Kate did.

'Fish is disgusting,' moaned Aoife. 'I want a burger.'

Aunt Kate took the fish away. Aoife waited. And waited. No burger came. No chips came either. Aoife sulked. Aunt Kate read her book. Aoife screamed. Aunt Kate put on her headphones. Aoife screamed until she was hoarse. Aunt Kate hummed to herself.

That night, Aoife went to bed hungry. She was very hungry and very upset. She hated Aunt Kate. Aunt Kate did not seem to care.

'Goodnight Aoife,' she said, tucking her into bed. Aoife said nothing.

The next day, Aunt Kate made Aoife potatoes, carrots and fish for dinner. Aoife's head said 'NO!' but her tummy said 'YES!'

So which won … her head or her tummy?

CHECK-UP

1. What did Aoife do when she did not get her way?
2. Why did Mammy go to hospital?
3. How did Aunt Kate react when Aoife refused to eat her dinner?
4. What was for dinner the next day?
5. Which part of Aoife won do you think? Explain your answer.

Footwear

There are many different types of shoe. Some types of shoe are very old. They have been worn by people for thousands of years. Other types of shoe are modern.

One of the oldest types of shoe is the **sandal**. These are open shoes with straps to keep them on your feet. Sandals are comfortable to wear in the summer time or for people living in a hot country. Long ago in Egypt, people used to make sandals out of palm leaves and **papyrus**.

Shoes are usually made of **leather**. Leather is made from animal skins. In the olden days, shoemakers made leather shoes by hand. This was very expensive. Often poor people went barefoot because they could not afford shoes. In Holland and some other countries in Europe, people used to carve shoes out of wood. These were called **clogs**.

Nowadays, shoes are usually made by machine. This makes them cheaper to make and cheaper to buy.

Shoes are not only made of leather. They can also be made of plastic, rubber, canvas and denim. You can even get snakeskin shoes! There are many different types of footwear. There are boots, high-heels, ballet shoes and runners. There are spikes for athletics. Divers use special shoes called flippers. There are walking shoes and football boots. The list goes on and on.

CHECK-UP
1 Name one of the oldest types of shoe.
2 What did the Egyptians use to make these shoes?
3 What is leather made from?
4 Why were shoes so expensive in the olden days?
5 Why are shoes cheaper nowadays?

WHEN NIGHT FALLS

By day, the countryside can seem quite empty and quiet. However, at night, it comes alive!

Foxes sleep during the day in their den. At night, they come out to hunt. They try to catch a rabbit or perhaps steal a chicken from the farmer. Town foxes like to root around in bins.

Owls sleep in the quiet old barns all day. When it gets dark, they wake up and listen. They can hear the smallest of sounds. An owl can hear a mouse moving in the grass. It will silently swoop down and catch its prey.

Bats sleep upside down. Their wings are wrapped around them like a blanket. At night, they wake up and dart through the air. They catch flies and insects of all sorts. Bats have very poor vision. However, they have excellent hearing. They use their hearing to avoid bumping into trees and walls.

Slugs, snails, caterpillars and all sorts of creepy-crawlies and mini-beasts come out to feed at night. All of the animals that like to eat them also come out to hunt. However, as soon as the sun peeps out in the morning, they creep back to their beds and nod off until the next night.

CHECK-UP
1. When do a lot of animals in the countryside wake up?
2. Where do foxes sleep?
3. Do owls have good hearing? Explain.
4. In what position do bats sleep?
5. What happens when the sun comes up?

Rosa Parks

For many years, black people were treated very badly in some states in America. They had very few civil rights. In the state of Alabama, black people had to give up their seats on a bus to white people. There were many other unfair laws against black people.

Rosa Parks was a black woman who lived in Montgomery in Alabama. On the 1st of December 1955, after a long day in work, she got on a bus to go home. She sat on one of the seats towards the front. When a white man got on the bus, the bus driver ordered Rosa to give her seat to the white man. He told her to go sit at the back of the bus.

This was not the first time this had happened. Rosa had had enough. So she just sat there and refused to budge. The police came and arrested Rosa. They put her in jail.

Soon everybody in the town heard about what had happened to Rosa. The black people decided that they would not travel on the buses anymore until the law was changed. Every day, the black people of Montgomery boycotted the buses. They walked long distances to and from work and school. The bus company was soon losing a lot of money.

After 381 days, the bus company had to accept the will of the people. They got rid of the unfair law against black people. However, that was just the start of changes for black people in America. Now they knew they had the power to change the laws if they stood together. Rosa Parks had made them believe anything was possible.

CHECK-UP

1. What law did black people have to obey on the buses?
2. Where did Rosa Parks sit on the bus one day?
3. What did the bus driver tell her to do? Why?
4. Why did Rosa not budge?
5. What did the police do?

Lamb

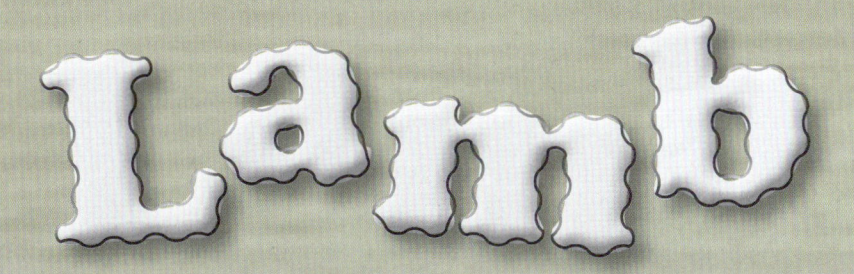

She was only a week old but already she was running and frisking around the field. The soft grass, the high ditch, the wide March sky and other sheep in the flock were all that she knew. Her thick, woolly coat kept her warm against the chilly March wind.

She had stayed very close to Mother for the first few days. Now she felt braver. She would go further and spend longer away from her. Even so, she would check now and again to see where Mother was. She could always tell which of the grazing sheep was Mother. No other sheep smelled like or sounded like her. In the same way, Mother could always tell her lamb from all the others.

She ran and frisked around the field with the other lambs. As she had fun, she was also making her legs and body stronger. She could dart, turn and twist with the best of them now.

Mother looked up. She saw that her lamb had gone further away than she wanted her to be. She gave a loud call, a **bleat**. The lamb heard her straight away. Time for her to run back for a drink of warm milk.

CHECK-UP

1 What animal is the 'star' of this story?
2 How old is she?
3 In what month of the year is the story set?
4 How was she able to tell her mother apart from the other sheep?
5 How did running and frisking help her?

Planets

The sun is a star with planets spinning around it. There are eight main planets and some baby, or **dwarf**, planets.

The nearest four planets to the sun are Mercury, Venus, Earth and Mars. These are called the rocky planets. That is because they are mostly made up of rock. Mercury is very close to the sun. Nothing can live there. Venus has air, but it is very thick and poisonous. Earth is our home. It is the only place where it is known that there is life. The air on Mars is very thin. Scientists think there might have been life there long ago.

The next four planets are Jupiter, Saturn, Uranus and Neptune. These are called the gas planets. They are very big and are made mostly of clouds of light gas. They have rings around them. Saturn's rings are famous. They are mainly made of ice water.

Further out in the solar system are the baby planets. These are smaller than the other planets. They are very cold and icy. Pluto is the first of these planets. Others are Ceres, Eris, Haumea and Makemake. The last four planets were found only a few years ago. There could be more baby planets out there waiting to be found.

CHECK-UP

1. What is the nearest planet to the sun?
2. What is it like on Venus?
3. What is the only planet where it is known that life exists?
4. Name the four gas planets.
5. What lies further away than the gas planets?

Postman on Sick Leave

There I was
Walking down the road
Slaving along
With my heavy load
When just after
I walk through a gate
I hear a growl
I hesitate.
Before I could turn
Poor old me
Some brute had bitten
Through my knee.
But as soon
As I get out of this plaster
I'm buying me
A canine blaster!

By Jim Halligan

CHECK-UP

1. What job was the man in the poem doing?
2. What happened to him?
3. What was the first sign of trouble?
4. Where did he get hurt?
5. What is he going to do when he gets better?

Yuri Gagarin

The first person in history to fly into space on a rocket was Yuri Gagarin. He was a brave pilot from Russia. Yuri was born in 1934 and grew up on a collective farm in Russia. One of his teachers was a pilot during the Second World War. Perhaps that is why Yuri wanted to become a pilot.

Yuri joined the air force in 1955 and trained to be a jet pilot. He quickly showed that he had great skill. When the Russians decided to send a man into space, they considered a group of pilots for the job. Yuri was in this group and passed lots of tests. He was not a very tall man. That may have been one reason why he was picked to fly in a tiny spacecraft called *Vostok 1*. Yuri trained very hard to prepare for the flight.

On the 12th of April 1961, *Vostok 1* blasted off into space. It was a very dangerous mission. Thankfully, Yuri got back to Earth safely. While he was in space, he looked out the window of his spacecraft. He was the first person ever to see our home planet from space.

'The Earth is blue. How wonderful! It is amazing,' he said through his radio back to Earth.

Yuri was very famous when he got back to Earth. Lots of people all over the world wanted to meet him. He visited lots of countries to talk about his flight. Sadly, in 1968, he was killed in a plane crash. The whole world was sorry to lose such a hero. ∎

CHECK-UP

1. Who was the first person to go into space?
2. Who might have influenced him to become a pilot?
3. Give one reason why he might have been chosen to go into space.
4. What was the name of his spacecraft?
5. What happened to him in 1968?

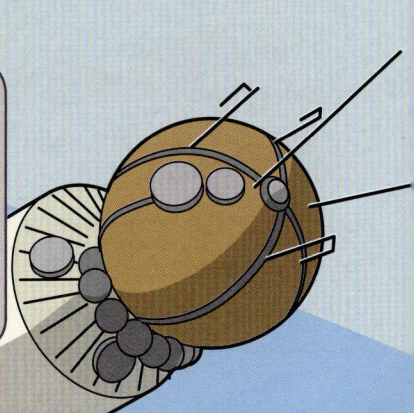

Rules!

Tom was having an argument with his best friend Paul about rules.

Tom hates rules. Bed by eight o'clock. Eat all of your vegetables or no pudding. Do your homework. Wear your uniform. Make your bed. Put your plate in the dishwasher. Put your rubbish in the bin. Practise the piano. Wear your coat. On and on the rules went. Tom was sick of them.

'But you need rules,' said Paul.

'No you don't,' argued Tom. 'When I grow up, I will have no rules for my children. They will do whatever they want!'

'Like run across the road without looking?' asked Paul.

'Well,' said Tom. 'I'd make a rule about that … obviously. I don't want them to get run over.'

'And they wouldn't have to brush their teeth ever, would they?' wondered Paul.

'Well … yes,' mumbled Tom. 'I don't want their teeth to go rotten.'

'And they could eat sweets all day, couldn't they?' said Paul.

'Not all day,' said Tom. 'I'd have to make a rule about that. They would get sick.'

'It sounds like a lot of rules!' laughed Paul.

'Alright. You win!' laughed Tom. 'We have to have some rules but it doesn't mean I have to like them!'

CHECK-UP

1. What were the friends arguing about?
2. What rules did Tom not like?
3. What rules would Tom have to make about crossing the road?
4. Who won the argument?
5. Do you agree with Paul? Explain.

Water, Water, Everywhere

Without water, there would be no life on Earth. More than two-thirds of Earth is covered in water. When we look at photographs of Earth from outer space, it is easy to see why it is often called the Blue Planet. Much of the human body is also made up of water!

Water comes in three forms: in liquid form (water), in solid form (ice) and as a gas (steam). To turn water into ice, it just needs to be frozen. When it is heated, it turns to steam. It is amazing.

Most of the water on Earth is found in the oceans and seas. This water is too salty to drink. Humans, animals and plants need fresh water in order to survive. This fresh water mostly comes from rivers, streams and lakes.

Water is needed for many things: to drink, to cook with, to wash with, to swim in and to play in. Farmers and gardeners need water to grow their crops. The oceans, seas, rivers and lakes are full of fish to be caught and eaten. It is very important that the water on Earth is kept clean. Dirty water causes diseases and fish can die in it. All life on Earth needs clean water to drink.

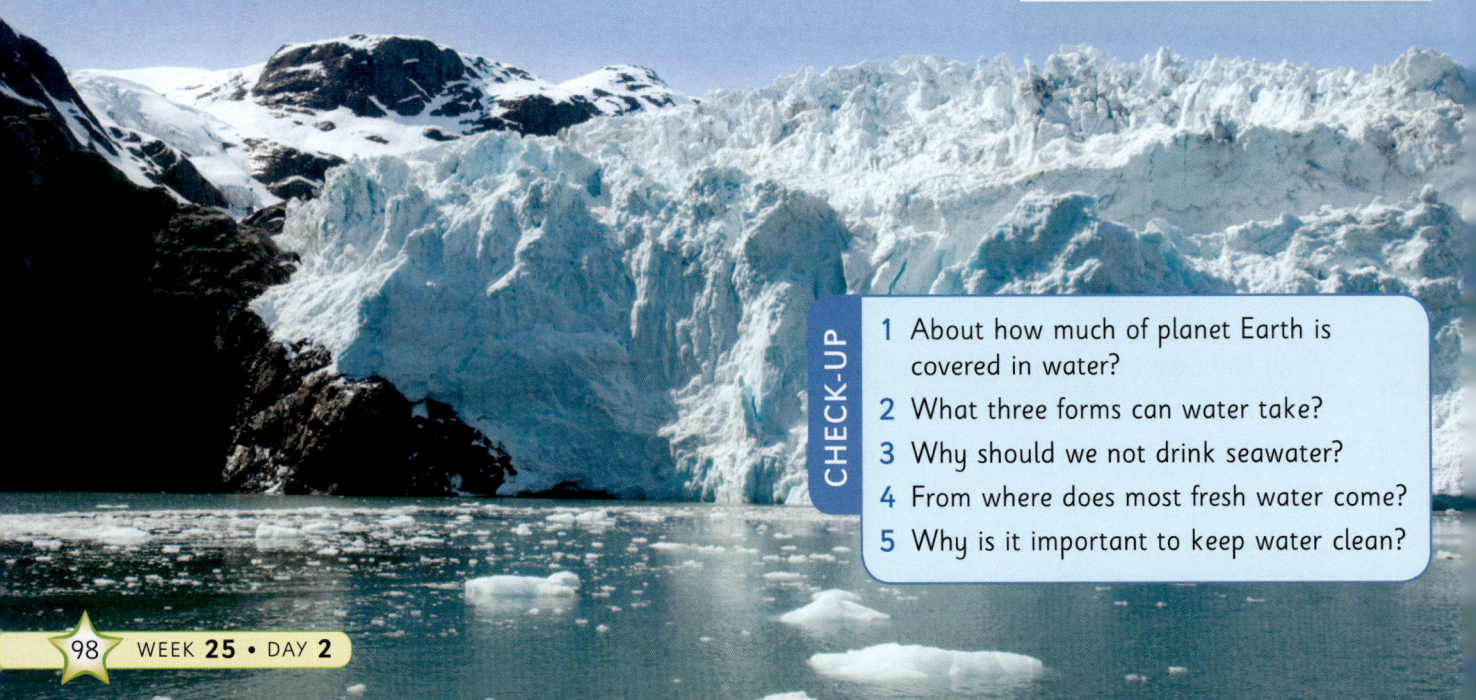

CHECK-UP

1. About how much of planet Earth is covered in water?
2. What three forms can water take?
3. Why should we not drink seawater?
4. From where does most fresh water come?
5. Why is it important to keep water clean?

Schoolitis

1
You haven't got a cough,
You haven't got mumps,
You haven't got a chill
Or any funny lumps.

2
You haven't got a tummy-ache,
You haven't got a fever,
You haven't got a runny nose
Or chicken-pox either.

3
You don't look a ruin,
You don't look a wreck,
You haven't got toothache
Or a pain in the neck.

4
You're as fit as a fiddle,
You're sound as a bell,
In fact I've never ever
Seen you looking so well!

5
You don't fool me,
I'm no fool.
Now up out of bed
AND OFF TO SCHOOL!

CHECK-UP
1. Name two illnesses that the child does not have.
2. What illness would cause 'funny lumps'?
3. What illness might cause spots?
4. Finish the phrase: 'as fit as a ____'.
5. Why do you think the child is trying to fool the parents?

Poem by Brian Patten.

William Tell

The national hero of Switzerland is a man called William Tell. He is said to have lived in the 14th century in a part of Switzerland called Uri. He was famous as an archer, having great skill with a crossbow.

At this time, Uri was being ruled by a cruel man called Gessler. One day, Gessler put his hat on a pole in the town. He ordered the people to bow before it as they passed. William Tell walked past the hat but he refused to bow. Gessler's soldiers arrested William and his young son.

The soldiers brought William Tell to see Gessler.

'I am told that you are the best archer in all of Switzerland,' said Gessler. 'If you can shoot an arrow through an apple placed on your son's head, you may go free.'

At first William Tell refused but his son said, 'Do it father. I trust you.'

William then put two arrows in his **quiver**. His son stood with his back to a tree. An apple was placed on his head.

'I am ready father,' said the brave boy.

William put an arrow in his crossbow, took careful aim and shot the arrow. It went clean through the apple. His son was unharmed.

'You may go free,' said Gessler to William. 'But first tell me why did you put two arrows in your quiver?'

William Tell turned to Gessler. 'If the first arrow had harmed as much as a hair on my son's head,' he said coldly, 'the second arrow would have gone straight through your heart.'

'You may go,' muttered Gessler, his face turning pale.

CHECK-UP

1. Where did William Tell live?
2. What skill was he famous for?
3. What fruit did William put on his son's head?
4. How many arrows did William put in the quiver?
5. Why do you think Gessler went pale?

Greenland

Long ago, in Viking times, a man called Eric the Red lived in Iceland. He had red hair and a terrible temper. One day, he got into a fight with his neighbour and killed him. Under Viking law at the time, Eric was banished from Iceland for three years for this crime. He gathered his family and everything he owned and set sail from Iceland.

They sailed west into unknown seas. After a few weeks, they arrived in a new land. Nobody else lived there. It was very cold but there were plenty of animals to hunt.

Under Viking law, any man who found a new land could claim it. If Eric could get other people to live in this new land, he would be their leader. After the three year banishment was up, he went back to Iceland to tell everybody about the wonderful place he had discovered. He called it Greenland to make it sound nice.

The name worked. People sailed back with him to begin a new life in Greenland. When they got there, they found that it was not quite as nice as they had been told. Even so, they stayed and Eric became their leader.

CHECK-UP
1 What colour was Eric's hair?
2 Was he a nice man? How do you know?
3 From which country did he set sail with his family?
4 What name did Eric give to the new land? Why?
5 When did he go back to Iceland with the news?

Travelling

Years ago, people did not travel much. The only way to get about was to walk or, if you were rich, to ride on a horse. The roads were terrible. The only ships were slow sailing ships. These needed the wind to move them. There were no aeroplanes or cars.

Times have changed since then. It is much easier to travel nowadays. People can travel from one end of the country to the other by car, bus or train. Big cities like Dublin have buses, trains and trams.

Ireland is an island. Because of this, people have to go to an airport or a port if they need to travel to another country. If they wish to fly, there are large airports in Dublin, Cork, Shannon and Belfast. There are also other smaller airports around the country.

Another way to travel to and from Ireland is by ship. Car ferries carry people, cars and trucks across the sea to Britain and France. Lots of people use the ferry to go on their holidays. Car ferries sail from ports like Rosslare in County Wexford, Dublin Port and Dún Laoghaire. ■

CHECK-UP

1. Was it easy to travel around long ago? Explain your answer.
2. How do people travel into and out of Ireland today?
3. Where are the larger Irish airports found?
4. What ways can people travel around big cities?
5. Name some car ferry ports in Ireland.

TYRANNOSAURUS REX

Tyrannosaurus were awful,
Tyrannosaurus were brutes.
No one could imagine
that Tyrannosaurus were cute.
Feet to squish you flat,
teeth as sharp as nails.
And if they didn't like you,
they'd bash you with their tails.
Wait behind a rock
for some poor passer by,
dig their claws and sink their teeth in,
blood and guts would fly.
Really messy eaters,
they probably had bad breath.
And if one should ever catch you,
that's it pal — it means death!

By Jim Halligan

CHECK-UP

1. Name all the ways that Tyrannosaurus rex (T. rex) could hurt you.
2. What could they do with their feet?
3. Why do you think they would hide behind a rock?
4. What would they use to kill their victim then?
5. Would it be a pretty sight? Explain your answer.
6. What would happen if a T. rex caught you?

TAJ MAHAL

More than 300 years ago, a great emperor called Shah Jahan ruled India. He was very powerful and rich. He loved his wife dearly. Her name was Mumtaz Mahal. When she died, Shah Jahan was very sad. He decided to build a beautiful palace to hold her grave. It was to be called the Taj Mahal.

It took over 22 years to build the Taj Mahal. More than 1,000 elephants were used to carry all the stones needed for the building. Thousands and thousands of men spent long hours working to build the palace.

The Taj Mahal is mostly made of a snow-white stone called **marble**. There are wonderful patterns in the walls and floors. These are made from about 28 different kinds of coloured stone.

It is said that Shah Jahan planned to build another palace like the Taj Mahal in black stone for his own grave. However, his sons grew very angry over the huge amount of money Shah Jahan was spending. They overthrew him and the black palace was never built.

The Taj Mahal sits in a beautiful garden with pools of water. People come from all over the world to see it. Some people say that it is the most beautiful building in the world.

CHECK-UP

1 Who was Shah Jahan?
2 What was his wife's name?
3 How long did it take to build the Taj Mahal?
4 How many kinds of coloured stone are used to make patterns?
5 Did Shah Jahan ever get to build the black palace? Why?

Supergirl

It's not easy being Tina – schoolgirl by day and Supergirl by night. All day in school it is work, work, work. And all evening it is homework, homework, homework.

Yesterday, as soon as her poor exhausted head hit the pillow, the Trouble-tracer started beeping. Tina squeezed the sleep out of her eyes and read:

'Trouble in No. 97, The Green.'

That was teacher's house! Tina jumped out of bed. She spun around once to change into her Supergirl suit. She pushed her window open and flew off into the night sky.

Smoke and flames were pouring out of the windows and roof of teacher's house. The fire brigade could be heard in the distance. Ms Belle was standing in the garden in her dressing gown.

She was screaming, 'My baby! My baby!' The neighbours held her back.

Supergirl flew through the blazing roof and quickly found the baby's bedroom. Flames were licking at the legs of the cot. Supergirl scooped up the baby in her arms and sped out the window with her. She handed the baby over to her hysterical mother. Then off she flew to her own bed.

'Supergirl saved my baby,' Ms Belle told her class the next day, as they all listened with open mouths. All except one girl who just couldn't stay awake and was quietly snoozing in the back row.

My baby! My baby!

CHECK-UP

1. What started beeping as soon as Tina went to bed?
2. Whose house was on fire?
3. Who stopped the teacher running into the house? Why?
4. How close was the fire to the baby?
5. Who was sleeping in class the next day? Why?

Spiders

All spiders have eight legs. Most have eight eyes too. On the back of their bodies, they have special tubes. These are called **spinnerets**. Spiders squirt very fine silk thread out of these spinnerets. They use this thread to make their cobwebs (1).

After making its cobweb, the spider will hide at the edge of it. When an insect flies into the cobweb, it becomes trapped. The spider then moves quickly across the cobweb. It sinks its fangs into the insect, squirting poison. The poison works quickly. Soon the insect stops struggling. The spider wraps it up in silk threads and eats it. This may sound cruel. However, without spiders, the world would be crawling with flies, wasps and other insects.

There are about 40,000 different species of spider in the world. One of the most famous is the big, hairy tarantula (2). Another unusual spider is the trapdoor spider (3). It hides in a hole in the ground. The hole is covered by a trapdoor made of silk. When an insect walks on the trapdoor, it falls into the trap.

The net-casting spider throws a sticky silk net over passing insects. The biggest spider in the world is the bird-eating spider. It can be as big as a frisbee.

CHECK-UP

1. How many legs do spiders have?
2. What are spinnerets?
3. What are spiders' cobwebs made of?
4. What does a spider squirt into its prey?
5. Describe a tarantula.

Odd Jobs

What do you want to be when you grow up? Why choose an ordinary job when you could choose one of these fabulous jobs?

- **A chocolate taste tester**: this has to be one of the greatest jobs in the world.
- **A knife-thrower's assistant**: a job for the very brave ... or very foolish.
- **A mermaid**: no, not a real one! This is an underwater performer. This job is most suitable for those who can hold their breath for a long time.
- **A doll doctor**: all those poor dolls who have lost their heads or eyes need to be looked after.
- **A dog food taster**: somebody has got to do it!
- **A Foley artist**: a Foley artist creates sound effects for radio and films using all sorts of odd stuff. This sounds like fun.
- **A crocodile wrangler**: just grab the crocodile by the tail and keep clear of those teeth! Easy. Anyone can do this job!
- **Egg inspector**: do you fancy checking eggs all day to make sure none with cracks get into the cartons? Is this the job for you?
- **A golf ball diver**: you could spend your life diving into lakes and water hazards on golf courses to find all those stray golf balls. Fancy that?
- **Forest fire lookout**: for those who like the quiet life. You spend all day on top of a tower staring out over the forest looking for tell tale smoke.
- **A pet detective**: you could be out there, day and night, searching for clues as to the whereabouts of missing pets.

Do you still want to be a teacher, a doctor or a shopkeeper?

Chocolate taste tester

Pet detective

Crocodile wrangler

CHECK-UP

1. For what job do you need to be able to hold your breath?
2. What does a Foley artist do?
3. What do you think is the best job on the list?
4. What do you think is the most boring job on the list?
5. What job would you like to have when you grow up?

The Little Dutch Boy

Holland is a flat country. The people who live there are called Dutch. The Dutch people have built huge **dykes** to stop the sea from rushing in over the land. This is the story of Hans Brinker, the little Dutch boy who saved the town of Haarlem from the sea.

Hans was eight years old. One day, his mother asked him to bring some cakes to a blind man who lived outside the town. Later that afternoon, Hans left the blind man's house and set off for home.

It had been raining heavily and the sea was high. As Hans walked along by the sea, he spotted a small hole in one of the dykes. The sea water was leaking through the hole. Hans knew that if the leak got bigger, the dyke could burst. Then the town could be washed away by the sea.

Hans shoved his finger into the small hole in the dyke. This stopped the leak but he could not move from there. He looked around for help but there was no one in that lonely place. It was starting to get dark. Hans shouted for help but nobody heard him. His arm grew cold and numb as night fell.

In the meantime, his mother was locking up the house for the night. Hans often stayed over in the blind man's house if it got too late, so she wasn't worried about him. All night long, Hans stood with his finger in the hole. He was frozen stiff and numb.

At daybreak, a farmer came along and rescued Hans. Before long, the leak in the dyke was fixed. Brave Hans was brought safely home to his mother. He will always be remembered for saving the town of Haarlem.

CHECK-UP

1 How old was Hans?
2 To whom was he bringing cakes?
3 What did Hans spot?
4 What town did Hans save?
5 How did Hans feel during the long night?

Climbing the Wall

He looked up at the wall. It was huge. It was huger than huge. It towered over him, the highest wall in town. It was time to begin.

The first handhold was a bit tricky but he was able to get his fingers into a crack between two bricks. He then pulled himself up. He found another good gap a bit further up and pulled himself up again. His feet scraped against the wall, trying to find somewhere to grip and push. On and on he went.

As he climbed, he thought of all the nasty things they had said to him.

'An egg-head like you couldn't do something like that!'

'You wouldn't dare do it. You're yellow in the middle!'

'Yeah, you're a chicken. Or you will be some day!'

Well, he'd show them. He pulled himself up higher and one hand reached the top of the wall. He was nearly there. With a last heave and grunt, he managed to get his tummy up onto the top of the wall. Then, he twisted himself around on his elbows until he could sit on it. He had done it!

No one would laugh at him now! No one would ever laugh at Humpty Dumpty again! He would be ... whooooops!

CHECK-UP

1 What kind of wall was it?
2 Where did he find the first handhold?
3 Why did he climb the wall?
4 How did he feel when he got to the top?
5 What was the climber's name?

The Eiffel Tower

In 1889, the people of Paris held a special fair to mark the 100th anniversary of the French Revolution. They wanted to show the whole world what French people were able to make and do. The fair was set up in the centre of Paris. There were giant tents with displays of lovely French food, drinks, clothes, bicycles and glass. One special building stood at the entrance to the whole fair. It was the Eiffel Tower, which was specially built for the occasion.

A great French builder named Gustave Eiffel was asked to design and build the world's tallest building for the fair. He had already built the Statue of Liberty in New York. To mark the special anniversary, he designed the huge tower. It took two years to complete the tower. It is made of cast iron pieces held together with strong bolts. At 324 metres, it was the world's tallest man-made structure until 1930. It was only supposed to stay up for 20 years, after which time it was to be taken down again.

When it was first built for the fair, a lot of people in Paris hated the tower! They said it was ugly. However, after a while they got used to it and became very proud of it. When the 20 years had passed, they wanted it to stay. And it did! It is now one of the most famous structures in the world and a major tourist attraction in Paris.

CHECK-UP
1. In what city is the Eiffel Tower?
2. When and why was it built?
3. Who designed and built the tower?
4. What other landmark did this person build?
5. Did the people grow to like the tower? How do you know?

Superman's Diary

MONDAY MAY 3rd
Woke up early. Had to save a lady from a burning house before breakfast. Stopped a ship from sinking near China. Saved a man from being eaten by a crocodile in Africa. Lost house keys. Had to fly all the way back to Africa to find them. Silly me!

TUESDAY MAY 4th
Big storm in Japan. Saved a bus full of children. Stopped for a sandwich in India. Volcano erupted in Iceland. Saved a village from the lava. Had to drop super suit off at the cleaners.

WEDNESDAY MAY 5th
Batman's birthday party! Lots of fun until we had to go and catch some bank robbers. Had a burger on the way back from the jail. Batman loved his present.

THURSDAY MAY 6th
Got a call from the President. More aliens from space trying to take over the planet. Zapped them with my eyes at full blast. They won't be back in a hurry!

FRIDAY MAY 7th
Saved a whale that was stuck on a beach. It was heavy! Saved two cats stuck in trees, one dog trapped in an old shed and a polar bear that escaped from a zoo. What is it with animals today?

SATURDAY MAY 8th
Another crazy day. Submarine got trapped under the sea. Saved all the sailors. Then saved another cat stuck up a tree.

SUNDAY MAY 9th
Went over to Spiderman's house for lunch. A nice, quiet day. Thank goodness!

CHECK-UP
1. How many days are in the diary?
2. What month is it?
3. On what day and where did a man have trouble with a crocodile?
4. How many cats did Superman save over the week?
5. What was his busiest day for saving animals?

The World's Biggest Omelette

Poor Humpty Dumpty! There he was in bits on the ground and all the king's horses and all the king's men could do was make a big omelette. However, it was not the biggest omelette ever made.

In 2002, a group of people in a town in Canada decided to raise money for the hospitals and sick people in the area. Someone had a great idea. What about making the world's biggest omelette? People would pay to see that! They got all of their friends to help. Local shops, farms and supermarkets helped too. It took weeks to get all the eggs collected. A special giant pan had to be made.

On the day, a huge crowd gathered in a hall to watch the omelette being made. The eggs were cracked into buckets and beaten. They were then poured into the giant pan. The pan had to stand on very strong legs with a special heater underneath. Nobody knew if they would be able to cook such a huge omelette. It took a very long time but, finally, it was ready.

When they checked how heavy it was, they found that the omelette weighed nearly three tonnes. That's as heavy as three cars! It was a new world record. Everybody was thrilled. There was one tiny problem: who was going to eat it?

CHECK-UP

1 Why did the people decide to make a giant omelette?
2 What did they have to do to get ready for the record?
3 What did they beat the eggs in?
4 Did many people come to see the omelette being cooked?
5 How heavy was the omelette?

Dream Catcher

Kevin was afraid to go asleep because he had nightmares every night.

'Tell me what you dream about,' Mammy asked one night, after he woke up again, shaking and crying. Kevin told her about his nightmare. But it sounded silly and not at all scary when he wasn't asleep.

'Oh, you are a silly Billy', she said. She gave him a kiss and tucked him into bed tightly. She then went back to her own bed.

But as soon as Kevin closed his eyes and fell asleep, his nightmares began again. In the morning, he was so tired that he fell asleep at school. This was becoming a real problem!

'For every problem, there is an answer,' said Granny, when Mammy told her about Kevin's nightmares.

Granny called Kevin over to her. 'Hang this over your bed and your nightmares will be no more,' she told him, handing him a dream catcher. A Native American man had given it to her when she was on holidays.

Kevin didn't think that the dream catcher would work. He hung it over his bed that night and went to sleep. And guess what? All the silly Billy nightmares were caught in the dream catcher net and only happy dreams got through. That night, Kevin slept like a baby!

CHECK-UP

1. What is the name of the story?
2. What was Kevin like after he woke up from a nightmare?
3. What happened to Kevin in school?
4. Who gave Kevin the dream catcher?
5. What does it mean 'to sleep like a baby'?

Lulu

Some things are funny when you look back on them, but were not funny at the time.

When Kate was three years old, she had an imaginary friend called Lulu. Lulu went everywhere with Kate – to the shops, to the crèche and to bed. Kate chatted and played with Lulu all day.

On the day of our holidays, we left very early. Kate was still asleep when Daddy lifted her into the car. Two hours later, she opened her eyes, took her thumb out of her mouth and asked: 'Where is Lulu?'

Nobody answered.

'We forgot Lulu?' she wailed. 'Poor Lulu is at home. All on her own!'

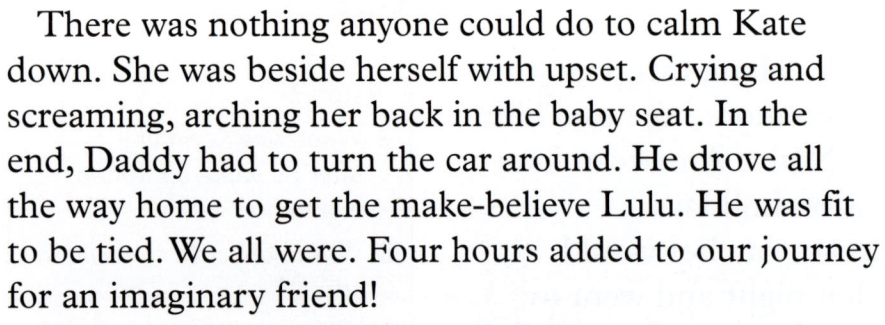

There was nothing anyone could do to calm Kate down. She was beside herself with upset. Crying and screaming, arching her back in the baby seat. In the end, Daddy had to turn the car around. He drove all the way home to get the make-believe Lulu. He was fit to be tied. We all were. Four hours added to our journey for an imaginary friend!

Kate is six years old now and she doesn't remember Lulu. When we tell her the story, she just shakes her head and laughs. 'You're making it up!' she laughs. It wasn't so funny at the time!

CHECK-UP

1. How old was Kate when she had an imaginary friend?
2. Where did Kate and Lulu go together?
3. For how many hours did Kate sleep in the car?
4. Should Daddy have driven back for Lulu? Talk about it.
5. In what way is it funny now but wasn't then?

The Sun

The nearest star to planet Earth is the sun. The sun is huge. However, it is not the biggest star in the sky. Many stars are much bigger than the sun. They just look so small because they are so far away.

Like all stars, the sun is a great ball of hot, burning gas. It is almost five billion years old. One day it will have burnt up all of its gas and will die. However, this will not happen for about another five billion years!

When the sun does begin to die, it will swell up to about 100 times its present size. Like all dying stars, it will turn into a **Red Giant**. Then it will get very small and become a **White Dwarf**. It will still be very hot and will take about another billion years to cool down. It will then be a **Black Dwarf**. It is thought that this will be no more than a cold black cinder. ∎

Choose the correct answer.

1 The nearest star to the Earth is:
  (a) the moon, (b) the sun or (c) Mercury.

2 The sun will burn out in about:
  (a) one million years, (b) one billion years or (c) five billion years.

3 A dying star first becomes:
  (a) a Black Dwarf, (b) a White Dwarf or (c) a Red Giant.

CHECK-UP

1 What is the title of this piece?
2 What is the nearest star to Earth?
3 Why does the sun look so much bigger than the other stars?
4 What are stars made of?
5 How long does it take for a White Dwarf to cool down?

The Lady of the Lamp

Florence Nightingale was born to an English family living in Florence, Italy, almost 200 years ago. Even as a child, she cared for others. She was always looking after sick cats and friends who did not feel well. When she was older, she decided to become a nurse.

Florence was a very kind and excellent nurse. In those days, nurses were hardly trained at all. They did not really know how to look after sick people. Florence changed all that. She helped many sick and dying soldiers. Sometimes she worked all night. She carried her lamp up and down the hospital wards to check on the sick. They nicknamed her 'The Lady of the Lamp'.

A terrible war broke out in Crimea in 1853. The hospital for the injured soldiers was filthy. It was overrun with rats. It did not have enough beds or clean blankets. Florence went to help in the hospital. It was very dangerous but she was very brave. She brought a team of the best nurses she could find with her. Florence and the other nurses worked day and night to clean the hospital. They got rid of the rats. They washed all the sheets and blankets. They put clean bandages on the injured soldiers' wounds. They cooked them proper meals. As a result, many injured soldiers returned to good health.

When the war was over, the Queen of England gave Florence a special award for her wonderful work. ■

CHECK-UP

1. Why was Florence Nightingale called 'The Lady of the Lamp'?
2. Describe the hospital where the injured soldiers were brought.
3. What changes did Florence make to the hospital?
4. Who gave Florence an award? Why?
5. Why do you think she was called 'Florence'?

Up in a Cloud

Dad and I were driving through the Wicklow Mountains. The road was winding and narrow. Mountain sheep watched us as we passed by. The sunshine faded into a hazy fog as the road got higher. It was getting misty. Dad pulled the car over to the side of the road.

'Come on. Hop out,' he said. 'This should be nice.'

'What?' I asked.

'Wait and see. Put your coat on.'

We got out of the car and walked down the road. I looked back. I could barely see the car. The mist was getting thicker. It was still bright though. The mist seemed to glow just a little bit.

It was so quiet! There wasn't a sound. Nothing stirred, nothing moved. We could have been the only people on the planet at that moment.

'Where are we?' I whispered.

'We're in a cloud,' said Dad.

Then we felt a soft, gentle breeze on our faces. The cloud began to move slowly. We could see it. The light began to get stronger. Soon, we were in full sunshine again. The cloud had passed.

'Cool?' asked Dad.

'Very cool,' I said.

We headed back to the car. ■

CHECK-UP
1 Who was in the car?
2 What animals did they see?
3 What was the road like?
4 What happened to the sunshine?
5 How do you know they liked what they saw?

MINES

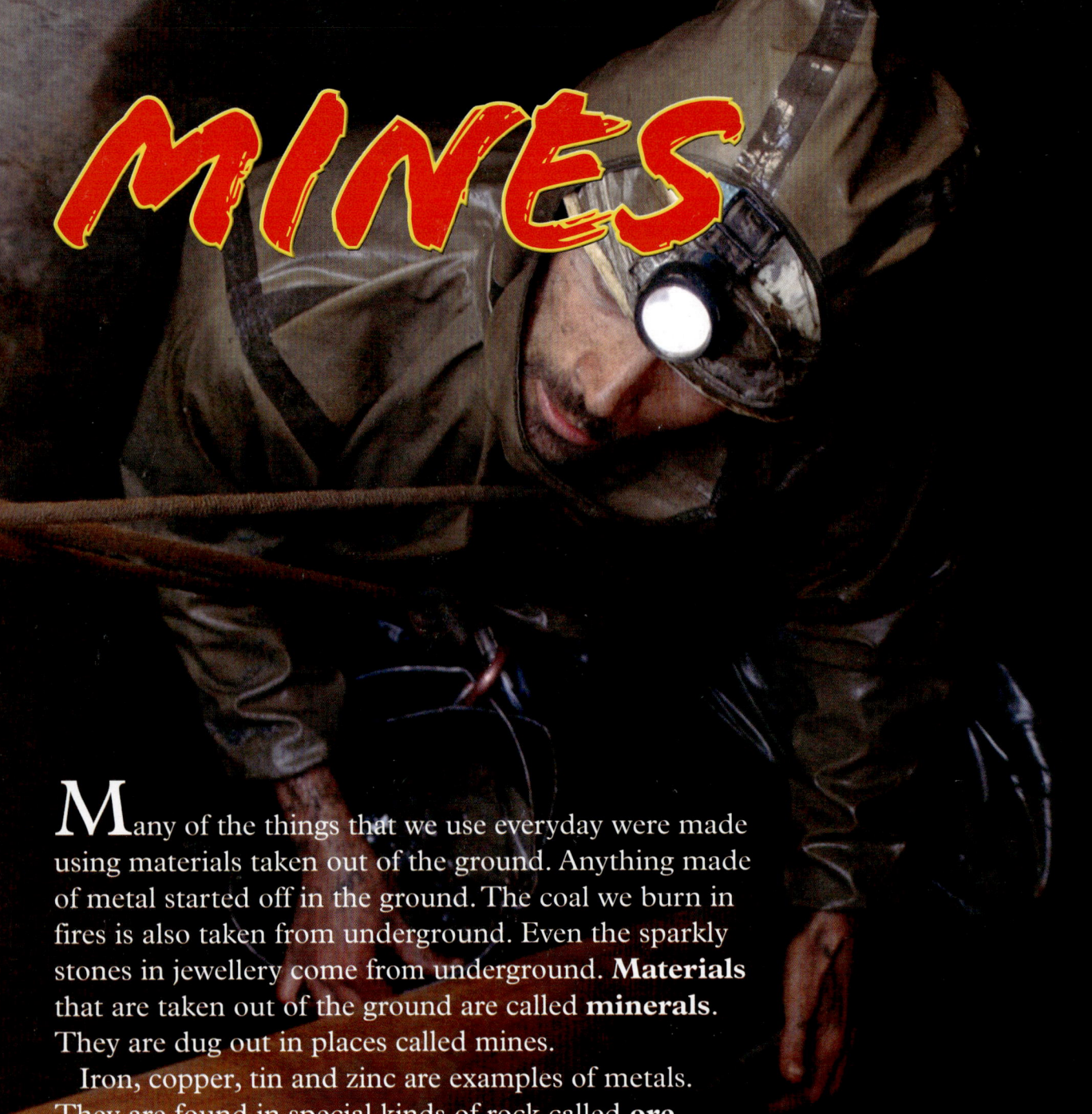

Many of the things that we use everyday were made using materials taken out of the ground. Anything made of metal started off in the ground. The coal we burn in fires is also taken from underground. Even the sparkly stones in jewellery come from underground. **Materials that are taken out of the ground are called minerals.** They are dug out in places called mines.

Iron, copper, tin and zinc are examples of metals. They are found in special kinds of rock called **ore**. **Ore** is not found everywhere. People and companies have to search carefully for ore.

Some mines are like huge holes with diggers scooping out lots of rock. Other mines use long, deep tunnels to go underground. The deepest mine tunnels in the world are in the diamond and gold mines of South Africa. The TauTona mineshaft is five kilometres deep. Some tunnels are so deep that they are warmed by heat from the Earth's core.

There have also been mines in Ireland. Metals like lead, zinc, copper and gold have all been mined here. ■

CHECK-UP

1 Where do metals come from?
2 What is an ore?
3 Are all mines made of tunnels? Explain.
4 Where are the world's deepest mines?
5 Name some metals that have been mined in Ireland.

Animal World Records

Largest mammal	Blue whale
Tallest land mammal	Giraffe
Heaviest land mammal	African elephant
Largest fish	Whale shark
Largest bird	Ostrich
Longest snake	Python
Fastest land animal	Cheetah
Fastest bird	Peregrine falcon
Fastest bird on land	Ostrich
Fastest fish	Sailfish
Smallest bird	Bee hummingbird
Slowest land mammal	Three-toed sloth
Largest insect	African goliath beetle
Largest reptile	Saltwater crocodile
Smallest mammal	Bumblebee bat (Kitti's hog-nosed bat)
Longest living land animal	Giant tortoise
Loudest sea animal	Blue whale
Most poisonous animal	Sea wasp jellyfish
Largest eye	Giant squid
Largest foot	Elephant
Largest teeth	Elephant
Longest tail	Giraffe
Longest tongue	Blue whale
Biggest ears	African elephant

CHECK-UP

1. How many records does the elephant hold?
2. Name the smallest mammal in the world.
3. Name the fastest land animal in the world.
4. Name all the world records for birds.
5. How many records are for animals from the sea?

Dublin Zoo

Dublin Zoo is one of the oldest zoos in the world. It is located in the Phoenix Park. It first opened in September 1831. It has changed a lot since then.

When it opened, the zoo had a lot of animals in small cages. They did not have much room to move about. The animals were not very happy. Over the years, the zoo keepers have learned a lot about how to care for animals. Today, Dublin Zoo is an excellent zoo and the animals are well cared for and happy. The animals live in large spaces. These are more like their homes in the wild.

One of the large spaces in the zoo is the African Plains area. African animals such as zebra are free to wander around this plain as they like. There is also a special forest trail for the elephants. Many of the monkeys live on their own special island in the lake.

Dublin Zoo looks after some very rare animals. It is home to rare fruit bats and Golden Lion Tamarins from South America. Without the work of the zoo, these animals could become **extinct**. This means that there would be none of them left in the world. Sometimes, the zoo swaps animals with other zoos. Then more rare animals can be bred. Lots of baby gorillas, chimpanzees and hippopotamuses have been born in the zoo.

Almost a million people visit Dublin Zoo every year. Maybe you will go there some day. ◼

CHECK-UP

1. When did Dublin Zoo open?
2. What were the animal cages like then?
3. Do you think this was good for the animals?
4. Where do many of the monkeys live?
5. Name some of the rare animals that the zoo is helping to protect.